This project was supported by Cooperative Agreement
Number 2003-HS-WX-K050 awarded by the Office
of Community Oriented Policing Services, U.S.
Department of Justice. Opinions contained in
this document are those of the authors and do not
necessarily represent the official position or policies of
the U.S. Department of Justice. References to specific
agencies, companies, products, or services should not
be considered an endorsement by the authors or the
U.S. Department of Justice. Rather, the references are
illustrations to supplement discussion of the issues.

This document is the result of collaboration among
several large law enforcement agencies. References to
the Internal Affairs methods or approaches of specific
agencies are included in the document as illustrative
examples only and should not be considered an
endorsement, recommendation, or favoring by the U.S.
Department of Justice.

For further information concerning this report, contact
Los Angeles Police Department
Commanding Officer, Professional Standards Bureau
304 South Broadway, Suite 200
Los Angeles, CA 90013
213.473.6672

Contents

Standards and Guidelines for Internal Affairs: Recommendations from a Community of Practice

Letter from the Director

Since 1996, and as part of our mission, the Office of Community Oriented Policing Services (the COPS Office) has been supporting law enforcement agencies in a variety of initiatives and programs to create or strengthen local programs that help agencies build trust with the communities they are sworn to serve and protect. The COPS Office seeks to create the community policing environments that develop or improve that trust and mutual respect and ensure equal treatment for all citizens.

Mutual trust and respect are at the heart of effective policing and the overwhelming majority of our nation's law enforcement officers are principled men and women who provide professional services to the communities they serve with honor and distinction. The responsibilities they shoulder are great, and agency and public expectations are high.

Unfortunately, on the rare occasion when an officer is accused of misconduct or criminal activity, he or she may be subject to an investigation. Implementing an honest and fair fact-finding process that uncovers the truth is the important role of the internal affairs function of a law enforcement agency, and it is essential to maintain a process that protects the rights of all involved, including the accused officer.

This report, *Standards and Guidelines for Internal Affairs: Recommendations from a Community of Practice,* was developed by the National Internal Affairs Community of Practice group, a collaborative partnership of the Los Angeles (California) Police Department and 11 other major city and county law enforcement agencies. The agencies shared and developed standards and best practices in internal affairs work, discussed differences and similarities in practice, and looked at various approaches to improving their individual and collective agencies' internal affairs practices.

The COPS Office understands the importance of learning from the experience of others. It is in this spirit that we are pleased to provide this report to you. We hope you will find this publication helpful in your local efforts, and we encourage you to share this publication, as well as your successes, with other law enforcement practitioners.

Sincerely,

Carl Peed
Former Director
The COPS Office

Acknowledgments

This final report was produced by the following project team, whose members are solely responsible for its contents:

Project Team Leader:
Deputy Chief Mark R. Perez, Los Angeles Police Department

Project Team:
Major Cerelyn Davis, Atlanta Police Department
Lieutenant Detective Robert Harrington, Boston Police Department
Assistant Deputy Superintendent Debra Kirby, Chicago Police Department
Deputy Chief Thomas Ward, Dallas Police Department
Commander Brian Stair, Detroit Police Department
Assistant Chief Michael Dirden, Houston Police Department
Captain Karyn Mannis, Los Angeles County Sheriff's Depatment
Major Donald Rifkin, Miami-Dade Police Department
Deputy Chief Bruce Adams, New Orleans Police Department
Inspector Robert Small, Philadelphia Police Department
Commander George Richards, Phoenix Police Department
Inspector Matthew Klein, Metropolitan Police Department (Washington, D.C.)

Special thanks to:
Chief Michael Berkow, Savannah-Chatham Metropolitan Police Department, who originated the project while working for the Los Angeles Police Department as Deputy Chief.

Senior Policy Analyst Albert A. Pearsall III, U.S. Department of Justice Office of Community Oriented Policing Services, who continually offered guidance and assistance at every stage.

Judith E. Beres, a contractor with the U.S. Department of Justice Office of Community Oriented Policing Services, for her final editing of this document.

Senior Policy Advisor Steven Edwards, U.S. Department of Justice Bureau of Justice Assistance, who likewise was vital to the project.

Nationally recognized expert advisors provided valuable insights from the realms of civilian oversight, academic research, and consultancy:

Merrick Bobb, President, Police Assessment Resource Center

Michael Gennaco, Chief Attorney, Los Angeles County Office of Independent Review

Andre Birotte, Inspector General, City of Los Angeles Board of Police Commissioners

Sam Pailca, Seattle Police Department Office of Professional Accountability

Joshua Ederheimer, Police Executive Research Forum

Dennis Nowicki, Police Consultant

Dr. Geoffrey Alpert, University of South Carolina

Robert H. Aaronson, Aaronson Law Offices

Particularly in the early and middle stages of the project, many contributed to the discourse and ideas:

Commander Jeffrey Noble, Irvine Police Department

Commander James F. Voge, Los Angeles Police Department

Chief William McSweeney, Los Angeles County Sheriff's Department

Deputy Chief Michael Ault, Las Vegas Metropolitan Police Department

Major Welcome Harris, Atlanta Police Department

Lieutenant Melvin Hendricks, Atlanta Police Department

Superintendent Albert Goslin, Boston Police Department

Lieutenant Frank Mancini, Boston Police Department

Cameron Selvey, Charlotte-Mecklenberg Police Department

Lieutenant Susan Clark, Chicago Police Department

Deputy Chief Calvin Cunigan, Dallas Police Department

Lieutenant Regina Smith, Dallas Police Department

Gary Tittle, Dallas Police Department

Sergeant James Weiss, Detroit Police Department

Kimberly Armstrong, Edmonton (Canada) Police Service

Captain David Gott, Houston Police Department

Commander Eric Smith, Los Angeles County Sheriff's Department

Lieutenant Michael Parker, Los Angeles County Sheriff's Department

Lieutenant Temple Carpenter, Miami-Dade Police Department

Lieutenant Carrie Mazelin, Monterey Park Police Department

Deputy Chief Marlon Defillo, New Orleans Police Department

Deputy Commissioner Richard Ross, Philadelphia Police Department

Captain Carol Scott-Abrams, Philadelphia Police Department

Lieutenant John Echols, Philadelphia Police Department

Assistant Chief Andy Anderson, Phoenix Police Department

Captain Steve Campbell, Phoenix Police Department
Captain Kim Humphries, Phoenix Police Department
Lieutenant Linda Johnson, Phoenix Police Department
Jerry Tidwell, San Francisco Police Department
Kieran Walshe, Victoria (Australia) Police Department
Maureen O'Connell, Metropolitan Police Department (Washington, D.C.)
Allison Hart, moderator of the first two large assemblies

Thanks to the staff who did all the behind-the-scenes work:
Senior Management Analyst Teri Dixon, Los Angeles Police Department,
    who from the inception of the grant coordinated resources and carried
    a huge portion of the administrative workload.
Matthew Barge, Police Assessment Resource Center
Lieutenant Paul Torrence, Los Angeles Police Department
Police Service Representative Larita Henderson, Los Angeles Police
    Department
Captain William Eaton, Los Angeles Police Department
Regana Sellars, Dallas Police Department

Introduction

On May 5, 2005, the Los Angeles Police Department was awarded a grant by the U.S. Department of Justice Office of Community Oriented Policing Services to convene and coordinate the National Internal Affairs Community of Practice group. The initial purpose of the National Internal Affairs group was to create an opportunity for major city police departments to come together in real time on an ongoing basis to share and develop standards and best practices in Internal Affairs work and share these products with the wider field of policing. In the end, the group learned considerably more. The group consisted of 12 major city and county police agencies in the United States. Many other agency[1] representatives and advisors contributed ideas and the dialog that ultimately shaped this document.

The group learned that even where we expected commonality in practice there was much more disparity than expected. We learned that the definitions of terms shared were not always universal. Where we assumed there would be shared definitions, the group found that the assumption was wrong. A large part of the time on this project was spent trying to agree on the terms common to each agency.

We also discovered that profound differences among state and local laws, collective bargaining agreements, and organizational and political cultures are factors in the struggle to reach commonality. There were also striking differences among the investigative models, processes, and structures among the participating agencies.

We learned that ensuring ethical conduct is an organizational responsibility, not just of Internal Affairs because Internal Affairs is not an isolated agency function. It is integral to a more complex interrelationship among entities within the agency that had not been seen as interrelated before. These include recruit and in-service training, risk managers, lawyers representing the agency in litigation, and agency members who interact with labor organizations.

The project reaffirmed that Internal Affairs serves two communities—law enforcement and the general public—and Internal Affairs is essential in building and maintaining mutual trust and respect between agencies and the public.

---

[1]Although the term "Agency" in this report intends to denote the local law enforcement entity responsible for the general policing of a city, county, township, or other politically autonomous local body, the principles of the procedures and findings herein will likely be applicable to law enforcement entities of other kinds.

We did find that we faced many common issues, including a lack of resources, lack of understanding of the Internal Affairs function by many members of the agencies and by the public, and the need to be able to continue the community of practice discourse begun in this project.

Despite the sometimes striking disparity among the methods, models, and other features of the various agencies' Internal Affairs processes (see the Appendix at the end of this document), the group was still able to find ways of effectively accomplishing the Internal Affairs mission in different ways.

Inevitably the question should be asked: why didn't the Internal Affairs community of practice come up with best practices the same way investigators of homicides and narcotics come up with best practices? What we found was that because Internal Affairs investigates police officers, a unique set of challenges is created that do not exist in typical criminal investigations. These challenges are not solved with technical solutions because the challenges are not merely technical. The challenges include the dynamics of state and local laws, employment rights, collective bargaining agreements, community relationships and expectations, and organizational and political cultures.

It was not a goal of the group to fashion rigid and confining rules or standards binding all American law enforcement agencies. Neither was it the goal to impose best practices that would create a single measuring stick with which to judge each agency. Rather, the effort focused on drafting a set of general principles and guidelines, around which consensus had taken shape, that articulate the fundamental presumptions and values underlying the role of Internal Affairs in contemporary American policing.

We remain confident that police departments, managed properly, have the capacity to police themselves in a manner that enhances public trust. We believe that agencies that objectively and thoroughly police themselves, yet are accountable to the public and civilian authority, are stronger than agencies policed from the outside where internal accountability is not a priority.

1.0 Intake

"Intake" denotes the process of receiving a complaint. There is a wide range of accepted intake practices. The range of practices flows from the political, legal, labor-relational, and other factors incidentally affecting agencies using them.

The widest possible net should be thrown open at intake to receive all complaints from all possible sources of complaint. While the procedures for investigation and resolution of these complaints may differ depending upon their nature, it is a recommended practice to take in all complaints. Moreover, complaints as a whole provide the agency with insight as to how it is perceived by the public. Law enforcement is not doing its job if the public as a whole or in part believes the police are not effective, ethical, or respectful.

Section Topics:

1.1   What a complaint is and who may file one.

1.2   How a complaint can be transmitted and what forms it can take.

1.3   Receiving complaints at agency facilities.

1.4   Availability of complaint forms or other means of filing complaints.

1.5   Dissuading complainants.

1.6   Tracking complaints.

1.7   Complaint acknowledgments.

1.8   Auditing complaint intake.

1.9   Complaints and lawsuits.

1.1 What a complaint is and who may file one. Each event of alleged inappropriate behavior is an allegation, whether reported verbally or by other depiction. A complaint is one or more allegations by any person that an employee of an agency, or the agency itself, has behaved inappropriately as defined by the person making the allegation. The person making the allegation is a complainant.

Commentary

Each agency should require that every complaint from the public be received and evaluated to determine the nature of the agency's response to the complaint. Because complaints can literally be anything from irrational statements to clear reports of criminal corruption, intelligent evaluation of each complaint at intake is crucial.

The complaint process from intake to final disposition should be clear to all involved, and should include at least a general description of the categories the agency uses to group complaints and the procedures for handling each category. The descriptions and procedures should be in writing and easily accessible to the public.

Employee complaints best resolvable beyond the realm of Internal Affairs[2] should be redirected to other areas of the agency as the nature of the complaint dictates (e.g., supervisory issues, personal grievances, employee disputes, etc.).

1.2 How a complaint can be transmitted and what forms it can take. To the extent permitted by law, a complaint should be received whether presented orally, in writing, or in some other reasonably intelligible form. The point is to make it as simple as reasonably possible for anyone, including an arrestee, to present a complaint without unnecessary burden. The public has a reasonable expectation that an agency presented with a complaint will act in good faith to accept it.

Public proceedings or filings in which declarations under oath reveal allegations of misconduct against an agency's employee should be considered sources of complaints when the allegations are brought to the attention of a member of the agency responsible for the intake of complaints.

---

[2]"Internal Affairs," denotes the entity or persons within an agency whose primary function is to investigate the conduct of agency personnel.

Nonsupervisory employees to whom a complaint is made should be required to summon a supervisory employee to receive the complaint. If a supervisor is not reasonably or practically available, the employee should explain to the complainant how to promptly meet with a supervisor and/or the process of filing a complaint. A supervisor receiving a complaint against another supervisor of similar rank should, when practical, summon a superior officer to receive the complaint.

Commentary

Nonsupervisory employees are ordinarily not trained to investigate complaints, not invested with the authority to do so, and may have conflicts of interest in accepting complaints against their peers. Likewise, a supervisor who receives a complaint against a peer or superior officer should as promptly as possible involve a superior officer in the complaint receipt process to avoid a conflict of interest. The most pressing conflict of interest to avoid is that of one employee investigating a complaint against a co-worker with whom the employee may have or benefit from a personal relationship.

1.3 Receiving complaints at agency facilities. An agency should receive complaints at any of its facilities ordinarily accessible to the public regardless of the assignment of the employee complained against. Where an agency can arrange to have complaints received and properly processed by local government officials at locations other than police facilities, the agency should do so.

Commentary

A complainant should have a wide choice of locations to file a complaint. Permitting nonpolice officials of an agency's local government (such as the city clerk, ombudsman, etc.) to accept complaints gives complainants neutral locations to present their complaints without fear. Such arrangements should include at least an understanding among the local officials that they need to promptly present the complainant information to the agency's Internal Affairs.

1.4 Availability of complaint forms or other means of filing complaints.

A public complaint form, or other means to file a complaint, should be available upon request at all units and patrol stations ordinarily accessible to the public. Information about how to file a complaint should be available at municipal offices and other appropriate identified locations. If an agency has a web site, an electronic version of the complaint form should be on the site, capable of being filled out and transmitted electronically. The means of collecting complaint information, whether via written forms or another specific mechanism, should capture all information necessary to initiate the intake of the complaint. Whenever practicable, a complainant should be provided with a copy of the initial intake complaint so that the complainant can verify that the facts as initially reported were accurately and completely received. If the information on such a complaint form is transferred to a different numbered and tracked document, such as an official internal form for registering complaints, the original complaint form should be retained and filed with the official form.

The complaint process should accommodate all languages spoken by a substantial proportion of residents of the region. Similarly, brochures explaining the procedure for the filing and investigation of complaints should be available in those languages wherever a complaint can be made. There should be signage in English and those other languages at each patrol station or other unit informing persons of their right to make a complaint and the availability of personnel to assist in the process.

Commentary

These practices are recommended to facilitate the making of a complaint and establish methods so that each complaint can be accounted for. While many agencies use dedicated forms for public use in making complaints, others accept letters of complaint or take verbal complaints via a dedicated process and thus have no such public complaint forms. Where agencies do not use dedicated forms, there must still be a specific, dedicated process for tracking complaints once received.

Because American cities and towns are increasingly multicultural and multilingual, agencies should consider acquiring resources to accommodate receiving and investigating complaints made in languages common in their jurisdictions.

1.5 Dissuading complainants. The public complaint process should not discourage, dishearten, or intimidate complainants or give them cause for fear. Unless required by law, a complaint need not be under oath or penalty of perjury. Unless required by law, no threats or warnings of prosecution or potential prosecution for filing a false complaint should be made orally or in writing to a complainant or potential complainant. Practices such as running warrant or immigration checks on complainants at intake solely because they are complainants should not be tolerated.

Commentary

Employees who in bad faith attempt to dissuade complainants from filing a complaint or who attempt to convince a complainant to withdraw his or her complaint should be subject to discipline. However, where an agency has an officially sanctioned and regulated mediation process available as an alternative to the complaint process, a good-faith offer to a complainant to enter the alternative process is encouraged.

State law may require a complaint to be signed and made under oath or penalty of perjury. State law also may require warnings of potential prosecution for filing false complaints.

1.6 Tracking complaints. Every complaint should be tracked through final disposition. The tracking system should be automated, where feasible, and capable of capturing in separate data fields information regarding the complaint important for case tracking. The tracking system should alert investigators and those responsible for management of the complaint process when deadlines are about to expire or have expired.

Commentary

A reliable complaint tracking system is a means not only of managing cases but of providing public accountability for the follow-through on intake complaints. Absent a tracking system, an agency has no way of efficiently verifying that its cases are properly assigned, that investigators are providing due diligence, or that cases have been completed. For jurisdictions where statutes of limitation apply to complaints, system-generated alerts warning of impending benchmark or statute deadlines can help prevent cases from falling outside statutory time limits and avoid the appearance of deliberate indifference.

An example of one efficient means of ensuring that complaints are tracked from inception through disposition is the use of one official, agency-authorized complaint form. Such forms should contain a unique identifier, such as a number, that allows them to be audited and tracked. All original, official complaint information forms, as well as the finalized investigation, should be housed according to clear written procedures including at least the location(s) of the files, security measures to protect them, and the authorizations required to access them.

1.7 Complaint acknowledgments. A written acknowledgment of a complaint or a receipt should be provided to the complainant in person or by mail or e-mail promptly and should be documented in a retrievable manner. It should include a reference number, complete synopsis of the complaint, and the identity of the investigator or other responsible person and his or her contact information.

In some agencies, a complainant orally states the subject matter of the complaint to law enforcement personnel who then put the complaint in writing. In such instances, there is a potential for inaccuracy or omission. The complainant should be permitted to review for accuracy any oral complaint reduced to writing by any agency personnel. The complainant should receive a copy of any such complaint. If a complainant appears in person, he or she should be provided the opportunity to review and correct what has been written. If the complainant calls in, the complaint should be read back to the complainant for review and correction.

Commentary

A complainant should be certain that the complaint has been taken down completely and accurately. The complainant should have written notice that a complaint has been received and how it will be handled. When practical, the name and contact phone number of the investigator responsible for the complainant's case should be provided to the complainant. This saves time for the complainant and the agency when the complainant has a need to speak with the investigator.

1.8 Auditing complaint intake. As a routine matter, an agency should conduct regular audits to verify that complaints are being taken properly and to ensure that all employees are adhering to agency rules and standards.

Commentary

Some agencies use video cameras or undercover officers posing as complainants to test the integrity of its processes for the intake of complaints. It is not uncommon for organizations concerned with civil rights to send individuals posing as complainants to conduct similar tests. Some complaint forms ask directly whether any attempt to intimidate the complainant has been made. However achieved, agencies should devise means to test whether the reporting systems function as designed and whether the employees trusted to operate the systems know what to do and are following the procedures in good faith.

1.9 Complaints and lawsuits. Complaints that are legal claims against the agency or any of its personnel for on- or off-duty conduct under color of authority should be coordinated with the agency's or city's risk management unit and the attorneys representing and defending the city in civil matters.

Any civil lawsuit or civil claim filed against a municipality, agency, or law enforcement personnel for misconduct on duty or off duty under color of authority should be handled as a complaint.

Agencies should consider creating rules requiring employees who are the subject of lawsuits alleging off-duty misconduct under color of authority to report the lawsuit without delay to their Internal Affairs unit or their commanding officer.

Commentary

Any lawsuit or claim that alleges misconduct, including those filed with another governmental or administrative agency, should be immediately brought to the attention of the agency's Internal Affairs unit or its equivalent. Unless the claim is investigated elsewhere within the agency's government, it should be processed as a complaint at intake.

A lawsuit alleging on-duty activities would ordinarily be served on the officer and employer, putting both on notice of the alleged facts. This is dealt with in an earlier section of this report. However, lawsuits regarding off-duty actions under color of authority may not only implicate employer liability, but may reveal that an officer has violated agency rules regarding off-duty behavior.

2.0 Classification of Complaints

Promptly upon intake, it is the responsibility of the Internal Affairs unit to classify the complaint for purposes of determining where, when, and how the complaint will be investigated and resolved. It is helpful to classify complaints into either of two categories: criminal or administrative. A complaint that is criminal is investigated quite differently from a complaint that is administrative. Criminal misconduct may lead to prosecution and jail or prison. An administrative complaint may lead only to internal discipline or other corrective action.

Some agencies break administrative complaints into subclassifications of personnel complaints and service complaints. Personnel complaints address alleged misconduct by an employee. Service complaints address problems in the provision of service not linked in any way to an employee's possible misconduct, such as a complaint that the agency's response times are routinely too long.

Section Topics:

2.1 Criminal complaints.

2.2 When criminal prosecution is declined.

2.3 Internal administrative complaints.

2.4 Holding administrative complaints in abeyance during criminal proceedings.

2.1 Criminal complaints. As soon as is practicable, complaints alleging possible criminal misconduct of an agency member should be separated, classified as a criminal complaint, and handled accordingly.

Criminal misconduct is when there is reasonable suspicion to believe that the agency member committed a crime. A decision not to classify a possibly criminal complaint as such should be approved by the unit commander of Internal Affairs or its equivalent or the agency head or designee according to protocols agreed upon with the District Attorney. If that concurrence is verbal, Internal Affairs should reduce it to writing and place it in the file. Declination of prosecution should not be the sole basis for closing the agency's administrative investigation associated with the criminal case.

Because agencies typically have rules making it an act of misconduct to commit a crime, agencies should consider creating rules requiring officers arrested or named as a principal to a crime to report that to their agency's Internal Affairs or to their commanding officer. Consideration should also be given to requiring employees who know that their fellow employee has been arrested or named as a criminal principal to report that fact to Internal Affairs or to their commanding officer.

Commentary

Questions arise whether complaints of excessive or unnecessary force must always be dealt with as a criminal complaint. A suggestion for a resolution of the question is that a complaint that alleges or suggests that an officer's use of force was willfully, intentionally, recklessly, or knowingly excessive or unreasonable should be classified and investigated as a criminal complaint. Some agencies have negotiated agreements over what complaints need to be prosecuted or presented to prosecutors for a decision on prosecution. It is recommended that each agency establish an explicitly codified protocol for the presentation of cases for potential prosecution. Any doubt or uncertainty with respect to a criminal classification should be resolved in consultation with the District Attorney or other local prosecutor.

2.2 When criminal prosecution is declined. An Internal Affairs administrative investigation should be opened to gather facts and determine whether there is sufficient evidence to take disciplinary employment action against an employee who is under investigation for a criminal matter. The declination by a prosecutor to proceed criminally or a dismissal of charges or a not guilty judgment or verdict should not lead to a termination of an administrative investigation given the nature of prosecutorial discretion and the differing standard of proof (beyond a reasonable doubt) and admissibility of evidence in criminal matters in contrast to civil liability or administrative proceedings (preponderance of the evidence). Evidence of an employee's plea of criminal guilt in court should be among the items collected and considered by an agency when conducting an administrative investigation associated with the employee's criminal case.

Commentary

A criminal investigation focuses on whether a crime has been committed and concentrates on the specific actions and mental state of the accused. An administrative investigation of a police officer, on the other hand, should look more broadly at the tactical, strategic, and training implications of a particular incident in conjunction with an examination of whether agency policy was violated. There should be an active administrative investigation of any matter that is also being pursued as a criminal investigation. The degree to which the two investigations should proceed in parallel or not is discussed at section 2.4.

2.3 Internal administrative complaints. A complaint made by an agency employee alleging criminal conduct of another agency employee should be promptly received and processed as a complaint by Internal Affairs. However, an employee's report of another's violation of administrative policies should be handled according to the policies of the agency, which could in many cases reasonably involve a process other than a complaint.

Commentary

That Internal Affairs should handle criminal allegations made by one employee against another is a generally agreed upon procedure. However, the policies and customs of agencies throughout the country concerning the way agency-specific administrative rule violations are handled vary greatly. Philosophies of internal discipline, leadership styles of agency heads, the discretion given to supervisors and commanding officers to determine how employee behavior is dealt with, and factors related to tracking potentially at-risk behaviors affect whether a complaint will ensue.

When determining whether to create a complaint based solely on an administrative agency rule violation, some important considerations which would tend to suggest a complaint include at least the following:

1. The employee has a history of behavior of a kind similar to the instant case.

2. The behavior appears to be invidious discrimination.

3. The act is a breach of ethics.

4. The agency rules require discharge if the allegation is true.

5. No less formal intervention is deemed likely to change the employee's behavior.

Conversely, where the conditions above do not exist and counseling, training, an employee development plan, remedial agreement, or other alternative to traditional discipline seem a reasonably worthwhile option, consideration should be given to dealing with internal matters creatively and without a complaint.

2.4 Holding administrative complaints in abeyance during criminal proceedings. Each agency should create a protocol for determining how to proceed with an administrative complaint while a criminal case based on the same facts is pending.

Commentary

It is common practice to hold an administrative investigation in abeyance during the pendency of a criminal investigation based on the same facts. It is often the desire of the prosecutor that the investigations be consecutive out of concern that compelled statements in the administrative investigation, if not handled carefully, may taint the criminal investigation. On the other hand, consecutive investigations can prejudice the administrative investigation. The time delay has a negative impact on the memory and availability of witnesses. It means that a cloud lingers over the employee for a long time. The longer eventual administrative discipline, retraining, or corrective action is postponed, the less effective and meaningful it will be. Moreover, a lengthy delay undermines public trust and confidence that the agency is efficient and is taking speedy action to remedy police misconduct, thereby increasing public cynicism about law enforcement taking care of its own. If an agency does conduct consecutive rather than concurrent investigations, the agency should keep the complainant informed as to the progress of the investigations on a regular basis.

Some agencies conduct contemporaneous criminal and administrative investigations. To do so eliminates the negative features of consecutive investigations described above. Contemporaneous investigations are more difficult to perform because of the strict necessity of keeping the two investigations separate. Additionally, contemporaneous investigations may involve double interviews of witnesses and a potential for conflicts in the record. Unless otherwise prohibited by law, the facts gathered in the criminal investigation can be shared with those conducting the administrative investigation; the reverse is not necessarily true.

Great caution must be exercised to avoid a compelled statement or the fruits of a compelled statement from leaking into the criminal investigation. To do otherwise risks losing the potential criminal prosecution because of constitutional violations of the privilege against self-incrimination. For example: Compelled statements should not be disclosed during the course of an administrative investigation. Just as in any investigation, it is bad investigative practice to permit witnesses to learn what other witnesses have said. Accordingly, no witness, including other agency officer witnesses, or other subjects, should be allowed to see a subject's compelled statement. And, Internal Affairs investigators should take care when interviewing witnesses, including agency officer witnesses, not to reveal the content of a compelled statement.

Prosecutors have discretion as to how much time it will take to decide whether to proceed criminally. In some particularly sensitive cases, prosecutors have been known to take a year or more to make this decision. In the interim, the internal administrative investigation is neglected. Memories grow stale. Discipline, if any, is long-delayed. Accordingly, some agencies proceed with the administrative investigation, including taking a compelled statement from the subject officer, before the prosecutor has made a decision. The prosecutor's views should be solicited in this regard and a collective decision should be made to best protect the interests of both the criminal and internal investigation.

3.0 Investigation

The guiding principle informing this section of the report is that all complaints made by members of the public and all internal complaints of a serious nature, as determined by the agency, must be investigated. The extensiveness of the investigation may vary from complaint to complaint commensurate with the seriousness and complexity of the case. Some small number may be capable of resolution after a cursory or truncated investigation.

No complaint investigation should be closed or otherwise terminated without the concurrence of the commander of Internal Affairs at minimum.

Internal Affairs should be the guarantor that every investigation undertaken by its agency of its own personnel fulfills its investigative mission. All reasonable steps should be taken to assure that every investigation is free from conflict of interest, bias, prejudice, or self-interest. Accordingly, investigations should, where reasonable and feasible, be conducted by an Internal Affairs unit that reports directly to the agency head or designated immediate subordinate deputy or assistant agency head. Agencies should have a policy to address any instance where Internal Affairs confronts a conflict of interest or believes that it cannot conduct an objective and unbiased investigation, such as when the agency head or Internal Affairs commander is the subject of the complaint.

Whenever it is necessary to delegate certain investigations to the field, Internal Affairs should monitor such investigations for quality and due diligence, and take appropriate action if either is lacking. Internal Affairs should be empowered to remand investigations to the field for further work until Internal Affairs has determined that the investigative quality meets its standards.

The rules and procedures for an investigation must be framed to ensure its integrity, thoroughness, and fairness. To the extent possible under state or local law or existing union contracts, investigations should be prompt and present no opportunities for the fabrication or distortion of testimony or evidence. The rights of officers under law or pursuant to union contracts should be carefully observed. Internal Affairs is responsible for upholding these rights while at the same time ensuring a timely and proper investigation.

In some Internal Affairs units, it is common practice for Internal Affairs to propose a finding to the ultimate decision-maker. Sometimes, Internal Affairs also proposes discipline to the ultimate decision-maker. In those agencies, the investigators are seen as closest to the facts and as professionals best positioned to weigh evidence and testimony. In those agencies, Internal Affairs plays a role in assuring the consistency, accuracy, and appropriateness of the disciplinary process.

In other Internal Affairs units, the role of the investigator is narrowly defined to producing a neutral, objective, and accurate factual summary. In such agencies, the ability of the chain of command or senior executives to act as judge and jury to find facts and impose discipline is highly valued. In such systems, great importance is placed on allowing unit commanders wide discretion over those they supervise directly or indirectly. Furthermore, in those agencies, there is a perceived risk that investigators may lose neutrality and objectivity if they are permitted to recommend findings or discipline.

Both systems have advantages and disadvantages. Either can be effective as long as Internal Affairs is required to produce a report containing all relevant and unbiased information needed to fulfill the agency's mission for the case.

Section Topics:

3.1 "Complete investigation" defined.

3.2 Frequent or chronic complainants.

3.3 Special needs of criminal investigations.

3.4 Cases Internal Affairs should investigate.

3.5 Cases Internal Affairs should relegate.

3.6 Recommendations for time limits.

3.7 The use of administrative leave.

3.8 Electronic recordings of interviews.

3.9 Standards of investigative report quality.

3.10 The use of a chronology.

3.11 Agencies should consider using compliance audits.

3.12 Response to, and review of, lethal-force investigations.

3.13 Lethal-force investigations: interviews and evidence.

3.14 Investigations during lawsuits.

3.15 Post-resignation investigations.

3.1 "Complete investigation" defined. A preliminary investigation should encompass an effort to gather key statements or evidence if reasonably attainable. The goal of a preliminary investigation is to determine if the complaint should be further investigated and, if so, by whom.

A "complete investigation" is one which includes all relevant information required to achieve the purpose of the inquiry. A complete investigation is not necessarily exhaustive. There are many inquiries where a good faith professional judgment determines that sufficient relevant evidence of all points of view has been acquired, and where collecting more information merely would be cumulative.

One should expect of a complete investigation that a competent adjudicator will be able to make a finding without resorting to surmise, prejudice, or assumption of facts at issue. A complete investigation should take place where the allegations, if true, would likely result in formal discipline. Likewise, a complete investigation should be considered if it appears from a preliminary review that an agency's policy, standard, or training may be a factor in unintended consequences apparent in the complaint.

Any decision not to proceed to a complete investigation should be made by the commander of Internal Affairs with a written explanation included in the file. Nonetheless, a small number of complaints will allege facts that defy science and reason and accordingly do not merit more than cursory investigation and should be closed with a finding that the complainant's claim was impossible to investigate because the allegations were physically, logically, or technically impossible under any reasonable construal. An example of such a claim would be that an agency's space satellite is continuously piercing the complainant's brain with laser beams, or that the agency's employees are stealing her internal organs from her every time she goes to the market. Complaints closed in this manner should be reviewed by the commander of Internal Affairs as a check against improper closure.

Commentary

Rules for complaint processing vary dramatically and for many reasons. Arriving at exactly one process applicable to all agencies in all cases appears to be impracticable. In general, agencies have to consider how much decision authority they are willing to repose in each part of the process, how much oversight they want to create to monitor the results of the exercise of that authority, and what counts as a complete investigation given at least the factors described above.

3.2 Frequent or chronic complainants. Some complaints are lodged by frequent complainants whose previous complaints have uniformly been found to lack a basis in fact. These complaints should not be summarily closed. A preliminary investigation, however, may be satisfactory to establish that the current complaint lacks a basis in fact or is a duplicate of facts alleged in another complaint. The complaint should be closed with a finding that there was no basis of fact or that it was a duplicate, after review by the Internal Affairs commander.

Commentary

So-called chronic complainants should not be dismissed out-of-hand. Persons who make unfounded reports on some occasions may accurately report misconduct on another. The predicament this creates can worsen as the number of unfounded complaints increases or the allegations become more dangerous if true. The following is a reasonable strategy to consider.

Where the number of unfounded complaints has gone beyond what is reasonable (20 or so within a year, for example), determine whether a pattern exists of reporting events that are one-on-one. If such a pattern exists, consider doing recorded covert audits of the complainant or of officers against whom the complainant has made allegations. If well-planned covert audits show that either the complainant lies or that the officers behave properly, these results should be considered when receiving future complaints from the same person. This is obviously very resource-intensive and, in fact, may be beyond the resources of some agencies. But it can be a resource saver if the complainant has become an extraordinary burden.

Other creative strategies should be sought. The point in creating a strategy to deal with a chronic complainant is to be reasonable about the strategy and its expectations, recognizing that whether every complaint is investigated exhaustively or each is handled as a merely patterned report, the agency assumes a risk of either wasting important resources or missing a true report among the noise of the false.

3.3 Special needs of criminal investigations. A criminal investigation of an agency employee, particularly one involving a felony or crime of moral turpitude, is so serious that an agency should consider extraordinary measures to ensure that the investigation is as thorough and independent of conflicts of interest as possible. Ideally, an Internal Affairs team trained in criminal investigations would handle such cases and answer only to the agency head or designee. If Internal Affairs does not have a criminal investigation team, another team of investigators should be selected for its objectivity, integrity, and skill to handle the case, and the team should answer only to the agency head or designee for the progress and findings of the case and determination of filing charges. Having investigators from the supervisory ranks would be desirable to avoid conflicts of interest, as would having investigators from a chain of command outside that of the accused employee if the accused is a supervisor or manager.

Commentary

Internal Affairs units typically report to the agency head or designee and thus have certain independence. In some agencies, there is a specialized unit within Internal Affairs dedicated to criminal investigations. In other agencies, certain criminal investigations are handled outside of Internal Affairs by a detective or homicide unit, particularly in cases of officer-involved shootings. In yet other agencies, the District Attorney may have investigators who conduct some or all criminal investigations and may present a matter to a grand jury. In some instances, an agency might ask another agency, such as the FBI, or an independent prosecutor, or a blue ribbon commission to conduct an independent, outside investigation or to monitor an internal investigation. From time to time, it has been proposed that certain sensitive investigations be conducted by a specially appointed independent prosecutor.

The goal in all instances is to ensure that the case is properly investigated and presented to the District Attorney for filing consideration. Further, the degree to which the public and the agency respect the conclusion of the case depends greatly on the agency's choice of investigative process and personnel.

3.4 Cases Internal Affairs should investigate. Internal Affairs should conduct all serious administrative investigations, including but not limited to officer-involved shootings, in-custody deaths, alleged constitutional violations, allegations of racial profiling or discriminatory policing or racial prejudice, dishonesty, drug use, sexual misconduct, cases handled for other jurisdictions, interagency cases, and cases referred directly by the agency head or command staff. Internal Affairs should also conduct all administrative investigations of allegations of misconduct that are likely to result in litigation against the agency or its members. Unless there is a specialized unit to handle internal complaints by employees of discrimination, sexual harassment, and other unlawful employment practices, Internal Affairs should conduct such investigations.

Internal Affairs should investigate all allegations of misconduct of command-level personnel with the exceptions of allegations against the agency head or in any instance where there is an apparent conflict of interest. A complaint against the agency head should be investigated by expert investigators outside the agency acquired by and operating under the auspices of the authority responsible for appointing the agency head.

Commentary

Certain internal investigations are sufficiently serious that they should be conducted by the Internal Affairs unit in order to produce an objective and competent investigation which the general public and members of the agency will accept as trustworthy and credible. Some smaller agencies without a full-time Internal Affairs unit should consider contracting with an independent external investigator on a case-by-case basis. So, too, should a larger agency to avoid actual or perceived conflicts of interest.

3.5 Cases Internal affairs should relegate. Investigations of less-serious allegations of misconduct by the rank and file should be conducted by investigators where the agency believes the investigations can be properly done. Complaints alleging simple discourtesy or rudeness, without any suggestion of discrimination against a particular person or group, could be investigated at the unit level. Similarly, complaints by the public regarding traffic citations and traffic enforcement could be investigated at the unit level. Internal or external allegations of minor infractions of agency regulations or policies, preventable traffic collisions, or minor performance issues also are appropriate for investigation at the unit level. Alleged excessive or unreasonable minor uses of force not involving death, serious injury, or hospital admittance or willful, intentional, reckless, or knowing misconduct may be appropriate for investigation at the unit level.

Internal Affairs should monitor field investigations for quality and due diligence, and take appropriate action if either is lacking. Internal Affairs should be empowered to remand investigations to the field for further work until Internal Affairs has determined that the investigative quality meets its standards.

Commentary

Because many investigations do not require the expertise of Internal Affairs investigators, assigning those investigations to the employee's chain of command for unit-level investigation can be an excellent resource saving. It can also reveal to an employee's chain of command information about the workplace and personnel that they would not know if they were not investigating the complaint. This benefit is often missed in assessing who will investigate a given complaint but should be seriously considered. Given that command officers and supervisors are accountable for their commands and their people, they should also be among the first to see complaints and get the first opportunity to act as leaders in resolving performance and behavior problems.

The absence of investigative expertise of local chain-of-command investigators can cause problems, however. Without the training and experience of Internal Affairs, local investigators may not produce the quality needed to fulfill the investigative mission. Time commitments to conduct administrative investigations by field supervisors may conflict with their primary responsibility of field supervision.

It is possible that the command officers in a chain of command can oversee such investigations adequately and remand for improvement substandard investigations. Yet consideration should be given to having Internal Affairs be the final judge of investigative quality with the final decision-making power to return to the chain of command substandard investigations for improvement. An advantage to having Internal Affairs manage investigative quality control is that it is most likely to provide increasing consistency and quality. Another advantage is that Internal Affairs' review of all complaints can reveal trends of investigative or leadership deficiencies that Internal Affairs can help resolve through agency-wide training.

3.6 Recommendations for time limits. Completion of Internal Affairs investigations should occur as rapidly as is reasonably necessary to fulfill the investigative mission. In all instances, however, an internal investigation should be completed within a reasonable time before any applicable statute of limitations or other bar to officer discipline has run out. It is preferable to conclude investigations within 180 days.

Commentary

Given localized statute requirements and wide variation in personnel and financial resources available to devote to Internal Affairs investigations, a specific, global standard for all agencies stating the time by which an internal investigation should be concluded is not feasible. Agencies with more limited staffing may, in good faith, require a longer duration of time for completing an investigation.

Statutory limits on investigative duration should be the minimum standard. Consideration should be given to the broader principles of the policy. It is valuable, for example, to complete investigations promptly out of respect to employees, recognizing that they suffer stress awaiting the disposition their case. It is also valuable to the development of public trust when citizens are notified that their complaints have been investigated promptly. There is value in taking swift corrective action to help a wayward employee avoid further problems. An agency can exploit the opportunity inherent in an investigative duration policy to enunciate broader principles which at once inspire prompt investigations and inspire respect for people.

3.7 The use of administrative leave. During the pendency of an internal investigation, an agency may place involved officers on administrative leave or reassignment should they be determined to pose a risk to themselves, the agency, or the community; should their presence become disruptive to the successful completion of the investigation; or if the agency determines that termination is likely.

Commentary

There often are legal restrictions on whether an agency can suspend with or without pay, reassign, remove peace officer's powers, or take other actions to prevent a peace officer under investigation from becoming a threat or liability during an investigation. While taking such actions may well be within the agency's management rights, no decision should be executed without reasonable justification. This standard helps protect the agency not only from legal attack, but forces the agency to avoid knee-jerk reactions to embarrassing or politically frightening events. It also helps avoid conflicts with labor unions. Finally, using a reasonable justification standard can show that the agency is as respectful of the law as it expects its employees to be, a notion that can accrue to the credibility of the agency's investigative conclusions.

3.8 Electronic recordings of interviews. Electronic recording of the live, word-for-word statements of all interviewees, including accused employees, is the best way to avoid interpretive errors in recounting statements. Except in covert operations, all recordings should be done with the full knowledge of everyone involved, with a lead-in statement by the primary investigator announcing the date, time, and location of the interview as well as the names and titles of everyone present. Asking each person in the interview room to self-identify can be helpful to auditors, stenographers, or others who may need to listen to the recording later and know who is talking.

Telephone interviews, for the same reasons, likewise should be recorded, with the understanding that privacy laws usually require explicit notice to all participants that the phone conversation is being recorded.

E-mail interrogatories are occasionally an option because the e-mails themselves become verbatim electronic records. They are most useful when the questioning to be done does not anticipate much follow-up. To use e-mail interrogatories successfully it is important to ensure that there is a means of authenticating the identity of the sender and the receiver, such as using only agency e-mail addresses where policies and practices prohibit employees from permitting access by persons other than the intended user.

Commentary

Whether an agency transcribes, summarizes, or paraphrases witness statements, electronic recordings are the best means of testing the accuracy of written accounts of interviews. As a form of quality and integrity control, audits comparing electronic recordings with written statements should be at least done randomly. Where variances are found, the cause should be determined and quickly cured. An investigator whose written statements vary often or greatly from the electronic recordings should be trained or removed as an investigator: the cost of allowing interpretive error or intentional misstatement can be of significant harm to the agency's integrity or reputation.

The question about whether video recording should be done occasionally arises. Practically it is more intrusive, more difficult to do in small areas, may require special lighting to be successful, and often requires special training to implement well. It is not necessarily more effective than pure audio recording in capturing all that is said.

One method of using video recordings that can be seen as helpful to both labor and management is in cases where the interviewee is being video recorded pointing to positions on a map, objects in a room, or otherwise physically re-creating an event that cannot be done fully in just words. When a video recording is done in good faith only for the purpose of creating an ostensive record that could not be created merely through audio, video recording can help the witness explain his account more richly so the investigators understand it more fully.

Absent exigent circumstances, as restricted by law or contract, agencies should give employees a reasonable amount of advance warning before an administrative interview in order for such employees to secure union or legal representation should they want it. Unless provided by law, an employee is not automatically entitled to any specific information or evidence prior to an interview or interrogation, though an agency may choose to make some information available to an employee and his or her representative prior to an interview or during an interview on a case-by-case basis.

Questions asked during the interview should be open-ended and non-leading. Those conducting interviews should take care not to formulate instantaneous credibility assessments that might bias the investigation. Investigators should receive ongoing training in interviewing and fact-finding techniques. Investigators should thoroughly cover in each officer interview what information concerning the incident the officer discussed or received from other officers or outside sources.

3.9 Standards of investigative report quality. The documentation of investigations must be thorough, complete, and as comprehensive as reasonably necessary. Using standardized forms or formats helps in quality control, evaluating comprehensiveness and sufficiency of content, consistency, and in recordkeeping.

Commentary

Knowing when an investigation is "as comprehensive as reasonably necessary" is the most basic but often the most difficult task of the investigation. At the least, the investigation has to answer the questions posed to it by the allegations. Beyond that, professional training, experience, and the resulting professional judgment governs at least part of the determination of investigative depth. Furthermore, the report should provide the decision-maker with enough information to arrive at a well-based finding.

Investigative Report Standards

To achieve the investigative mission, each investigative report should meet these minimum standards:

1. All allegations are clearly stated and clearly answered.

2. All relevant facts bearing on the truth of each allegation are clearly stated.

3. All evidence (e.g., photos, recordings, etc.) is included or its means of retrieval specified.

4. Contact and identification information for all persons interviewed and for the investigator(s) is included.

5. The report is impartial, with no bias for or against any party.

Beyond minimum standards, consideration should be given to assessing report quality according to at least these standards:

1. The report is logically organized with the aim of helping the reader understand it.

2. Its language is clear, and where special terms of art are used, they are defined. The reader should not have to presume or guess the meaning of a term.

3. It avoids conclusionary statements wherever possible.

4. Sentences and paragraphs are direct, simple, and easy to understand, using the fewest words to clearly convey the point.

5. Estimates of time, distance, or other quantities should be as precise as reasonably useful, but need not be precise beyond that.

6. Unless explicitly permitted by agency policy, personal opinions should be avoided. If they are permitted, they should include explicit evidence to support the opinion.

Standardized Forms

Standardized forms and formats have advantages and disadvantages. Basic forms, such as the intake complaint form, fare well having essential information required on them, such as names, dates, locations, contact information, etc. Formats for the investigative narratives and adjudication documents can also be helpful in creating a template for investigators and agency auditors to use to ensure that crucial information is included and is adequate. Consideration should be given to allowing some variation in formats so that information not ordinarily included can be if it needs to be. Simply adding an optional heading of "Additional Information" into any format can achieve this.

Each investigative report should contain a detailed, comprehensive summary. Although the summary should be impartial, it should also identify inconsistencies between statements and inconsistencies between statements and physical evidence.

3.10 The use of a chronology. Internal Affairs should track and maintain a chronological log of all internal investigations. A log of the investigation serves to preserve and maintain a history of the investigation and a means to keep track of the various parts of the investigation.

Commentary

A sound investigative practice common to investigations includes the use of a chronological log in which investigators make entries as they advance their investigations. Such a log would typically have entries of the dates, times, and contact information of each person the investigators called, interviewed, or attempted to call or interview. The log would include dates/times/contact information when items were sent for analysis. Any event that would evince investigative due diligence should be logged, particularly in jurisdictions with statutes of limitations or where complaint investigations are subject to discovery in legal proceedings.

Logs allow supervisors to determine the effectiveness of their investigators and also helps other investigators take over a case when the original investigator is on leave or is removed from the case. Whether to exhibit and track due diligence or to ensure investigative quality and continuity, a chronological log is a simple, effective investigation management tool that takes little time but offers great benefits.

3.11 Agencies should consider using Compliance Audits.

A Compliance Audit is a live test to determine whether policies are being followed. For example, a Compliance Audit of an agency's policy to document all complaints could be done by having someone call in a complaint and later see if the complaint was documented. Sending a letter alleging misconduct to the agency and determining whether a complaint was produced would also be considered a Compliance Audit.

Another example of a Compliance Audit is one in which undercover officers, or operatives, unknown to the on-duty officers pose as citizens, victims, or suspected criminals to determine how on-duty officers treat the public in various controlled conditions. These typically are video- or audio-recorded and include a substantial support team to ensure the secrecy of the operation and the safety of everyone involved. Compliance Audits can be quite complicated and resource-intensive, and typically require skilled, experienced undercover operators intensively overseen by supervisors with similar experience and skill.

Commentary

Where an agency has the resources to conduct them, Compliance Audits can help the agency detect misconduct before the misconduct is complained of by the public. Compliance Audits can also help pinpoint weaknesses in systems, policies, or personnel before anyone is ever accused of misconduct. Conversely, where well-done Compliance Audits continually show that the agency's personnel and policies are working well, this information can be useful in defending against pattern-and-practice lawsuits, and can argue against some deliberate indifference claims by plaintiffs.

The use of Compliance Audits lets the public know that the agency takes its integrity seriously. While the specific details of each Compliance Audit should be kept secret to avoid compromising tactics or methods that may be used again, publicizing the fact that an agency conducts Compliance Audits can help inspire public trust, especially in jurisdictions with a history of reputed abuses by agency officers.

Compliance Audits give agency employees the understanding that they are not above testing, helping to keep honest people honest. This is not always received well by employees, however. In some agencies, the advent of Compliance Audits brought complaints from labor unions that management was out to get their members or that employees would stop working for fear of being caught up in a poorly designed or poorly executed audit. Such comments have some merit, insofar as agencies who design and execute their Compliance Audits in bad faith hoping merely to prove their worth by catching someone risk the very problem some unions have claimed: employees may simply slow or shut down to avoid getting caught in a bad-faith trap.

One way of avoiding the worst of the employee relations problems created by Compliance Audits is to design them so that an employee acting reasonably, albeit not perfectly, would not suffer significant penalty for an error. If Compliance Audits are set up to ascertain ethical integrity, careful consideration should be given to whether some minor infraction would even be mentioned outside the Compliance Audit unit. If employees continually get penalized for minor infractions in Compliance Audits designed to catch corruption, Compliance Audits can be sources of employee bitterness. But if the only products of Compliance Audits are the detection of acts which are universally known to be egregious, the Compliance Audits will gain a reputation for catching only those whom everyone knows should be fired.

It is not trivial to ask whether, in a Compliance Audit, an employee should be rewarded when caught doing the job well. In one large agency, employees receive a commendatory document when they have not merely passed an audit, but have done an exemplary job. These commendations are not handed out often, but when they are, they are issued months after the event, the facts are not specified, and the date of the Compliance Audit is not given so as to avoid having the employees detect the undercover operators and their methods and expose them later.

Unit Leadership and Confidentiality

The selection of the Compliance Audit unit leader is crucial, as the judgment of the leader in setting up and responding to employee behaviors in the Compliance Audits is crucial to the reputation of such audits throughout the agency. The Compliance Audit unit leader should operate under, and be able to speak confidentially with, the agency head or the Internal Affairs commander to ensure that his judgment and actions remain consonant with agency doctrine. The leader would also have to have a high level of skill in selecting the right people for the unit and quickly removing those who are not right.

The practices and methods of Compliance Audits are beyond the scope of this document. But agencies seriously considering the creation of a unit to perform these kinds of integrity checks should spend the time to research the units of large agencies with expertise in the complexities of establishing and running them (such as New York Police Department and the Los Angeles Police Department). The smaller the agency, the more difficult it is to create such units without the use of personnel from other agencies because with agencies small enough for everyone to know each other, there is no anonymous undercover pool from which to pick. A solution is to collaborate with other agencies to bring in unknown undercover officers to perform Compliance Audits if the protocols, methods, and tactics are well-designed and universally applied. A written memorandum of agreement or similar document signed by and trained through all involved agencies can be extremely useful when interagency personnel exchanges are involved, especially if the agencies are from different government levels (e.g., state and local, or local and federal).

3.12 Response to, and review of, lethal-force investigations. All officer-involved shootings targeting or striking a human being, all in-custody deaths, and all serious uses of force as defined by the agency should generate an immediate response to the scene and an investigation conducted by Internal Affairs, or a team of investigators with special training in the investigation of officer-involved uses of deadly force, regardless of whether a complaint will be filed.

An administrative review, independent of any complaint, of a shooting, in-custody death, or serious use of force should consider the strategic, tactical, policy, training, and risk management implications of any such incident, including whether changes to policy, procedures, equipment, or training might mitigate the effects or reduce the number of similar incidents in the future.

To encourage the greatest degree of candor and revelation and to the extent permitted by law, the review should be handled as a confidential self-critical analysis and should occur in each case regardless of whether there criminal or disciplinary charges are made.

Commentary

There are multiple, concurrent purposes for an agency's investigation of its officers' serious use of force as defined by the agency. First is to determine whether the officer used force lawfully. Next is to determine whether the use of force was within agency policy. Finally, the investigation offers the agency a unique opportunity to review every feature of its personnel, policies, training, and other organizational practices that affect or are affected by officers' serious use of force.

Question of Lawfulness

An investigation that fails to provide the necessary relevant facts to allow a prosecutor to correctly determine whether the officer's use of deadly force was legally justified has failed its investigative mission. The public and the agency's officers expect that at minimum every agency will investigate to provide sufficient evidence to either prosecute the officer or to clear the officer of criminal liability.

Question of Procedural Compliance

A serious force investigation should provide enough evidence to determine whether the use of force complied with agency rules. In cases of agency rule violations, it can be helpful to the employee and the agency to have facts clearly stated in a report so that the internal follow-up actions will be properly justified and understood. An investigation that comprehends both the legal and procedural considerations is optimal.

Self-Critical Analysis

A serious use of force rigorously and candidly examined as a confidential self-critical analysis can be viewed as a research project with the aim of determining agency best practices throughout its systems, policies, and personnel by studying successes and failures in their real-world implementation. A serious use of force is a real-world test not only of that agency's organizational rules and systems, but can be a test of the theories and principles underlying them. There are few opportunities like officers' serious uses of force where so much can be learned from the exhaustive investigations typically conducted and expected.

It is important to consider that those who conduct such post-event analyses should include those in training, risk management, and all other agency units where the agency can draw on expertise to contribute to the discussion and analysis. The agency should seriously consider including not just high-ranking policy makers in these self-critical analyses, but also the practitioners at the lowest levels of the organization who know exactly and really what is taught and performed in the field. Outside experts can occasionally be helpful in this regard for special circumstances or questions beyond the expertise of the agency's personnel. In all cases the participants should be explicitly held to a standard of confidentiality such that the content of the discussions are not released to anyone but the agency head or designee.

3.13 Lethal-force investigations: interviews and evidence. The process of investigating an agency member's use of lethal force requires an extraordinary degree of attention to capturing and recording the statements of each participant and witness independently, accurately, and as soon as conditions allow.

Commentary

Given the disparity in the law across the country, in this section and throughout this document, agencies are best advised to consult with legal counsel about the applicable rules before implementation.

Unless otherwise required by law and without regard to whether the investigation is conducted by Internal Affairs or another specialized unit involved, witness officers should be physically separated as soon as possible to avoid even the appearance of collusion. Likewise, members of the agency either involved in or witnessing the critical incident should be ordered not to discuss the incident among themselves until after interviews of all involved agency members have been concluded and the employees have been explicitly authorized to discuss the matter. Where law permits, the officers should be compelled to submit to a comprehensive, electronically audio-recorded interview by agency investigators as soon as is practical and reasonable. Except for the Public Safety Statement (see below), members who were involved in or witnessed the incident in question should be permitted a reasonable amount of time to consult individually with legal counsel or a labor representative telephonically or in person before providing an interview with agency investigators. For some agencies, a "reasonable amount of time" can be as much as 3 to 5 hours or more. The point is to balance the employees' right to representation with the agency's responsibility to conduct its investigation without deleterious delay.

To prevent incidental collusion, members involved in or witnessing the incident should not be permitted to consult with legal counsel or labor representatives collectively or in groups: for example, two or more members should not be consulting in a group together at the same time with the same lawyer or labor representative.

Public Safety Statement

A Public Safety Statement is a statement made by an agency member involved in a lethal-force incident to a first-responder supervisor who was not involved in the incident, the purpose of which is to enable the supervisor to determine what immediate action is needed to find and protect injured persons, identify and apprehend the suspect, locate witnesses, protect the scene and its evidence, identify witnesses, and otherwise manage the emergency. Where the law permits, an agency employee is ordered to give the statement and is not permitted to await representation or refuse to make the statement. The first—or at least one of the first—uninvolved supervisor on scene orders the Public Safety Statements as soon as possible as part of his or her emergency management duties, and ideally would note the information to avoid error in the transmission of the information if needed. Once the emergency and tactical matters have been resolved, questioning of the officers is no longer part of the Public Safety Statement. Below is a set of questions one agency expects first-responder supervisors to ask in their Public Safety Statement transactions:

1. Were you involved in an officer-involved shooting?

2. How many rounds did you fire and in what direction did you fire them?

3. Where were you when you fired them?

4. Did any other officers fire any rounds? If so, whom, and where were they when they fired?

5. Is it possible the suspect fired rounds at you? If so, from what direction were the rounds fired?

6. Are there any suspects outstanding? If so, describe them, their direction and mode of travel, and how long ago they left. What crime(s) are they wanted for? What are they armed with?

7. Is anyone injured? If so, where is he or she?

8. Who witnessed this? Where can we find them?

9. Are there any weapons or evidence that need to be secured and protected? If so, where are they?

Once the emergency is resolved to a static protected scene, the involved employees are ordered not to discuss the incident with anyone except the investigators or their legal representative.

The answers to the Public Safety Statement questions help determine where unseen victims might be: asking where the rounds were fired, for example, allows an immediate area search for places outside the limited shooting scene where stray bullets could have struck bystanders in their homes. Knowing the armament, description, and flight mode of a suspect have obvious emergency utility. All the questions are designed to acquire crucial emergency information without the delay or depth of information formal interviews require. That is why, in many jurisdictions, the Public Safety Statement is compelled. If officers were allowed to remain silent, human life could be lost or harmed and criminal evidence could be compromised or lost.

The investigation team should participate in all scene walk-throughs with involved or witness officers. The practice of some investigators to conduct unrecorded "pre-interviews" of officers or witnesses prior to formal, electronically recorded interviews should be discouraged, but the practice of some agencies to solicit and obtain voluntary statements from officers should be encouraged.

In those agencies conducting contemporaneous criminal and administrative review or investigation, the criminal and administrative investigators should be empowered, should they choose and to the extent practicable, to conduct joint criminal-administrative interviews of all witnesses, including interviews of members of the agency and the general public. Similarly, where law permits, administrative investigators should be empowered, should they choose, to take a compelled statement from the subject officer or officers before or after the criminal investigation as long as great care is taken not to contaminate or compromise the criminal investigation. In any event, the electronic recordings from the criminal interview and, if possible, a transcript of them should be provided to the administrative investigators as soon as practicable.

In addition to documenting statements, sound investigative practices include the prompt seizure, preservation, and characterization of physical evidence and the most accurate depiction of the scene, its physical dimensions and the positions of all items of physical evidence relative to the time and place force was used.

3.14 Investigations during lawsuits. Each agency should decide as soon as practicable in each case whether the complaint investigation will be completed before or after a lawsuit on the same set of facts is concluded. Because the possible financial, legal, or political consequences of the decision could be extraordinary, the decision should be made by the agency head or designee.

Commentary

It is common in some agencies to hold an administrative investigation in abeyance during the pendency of civil litigation arising out of the same set of facts. Defense counsel fear conflicts in testimony between administrative interviews and deposition or trial testimony. Defense counsel also worries that the imposition of administrative discipline or a finding that a given officer's actions were out of policy or unjustified will prejudice the outcome of the civil litigation.

On the other hand, completing an internal investigation in as timely a manner as is reasonable, regardless of outside legal proceedings, helps the agency promptly find, and if necessary, resolve the questions or problems underlying the civil claims. The negative aspects of consecutive criminal and administrative investigations apply with equal force: witnesses' memories fade or the witness becomes unavailable; a cloud hangs over the head of the employee; eventual discipline, retraining, or corrective action is less meaningful with the passage of time; and the credibility of the agency in dealing with misconduct is undermined. Accordingly, some agencies proceed with the administrative investigation, including taking a compelled statement from the subject officer, before the civil litigation is final. The views of the agency's defense counsel in this regard should be solicited but should not necessarily be controlling.

Civil discovery and trial may create a fuller and more complete record than typical administrative investigations. Agencies should review, and consider reopening, an internal investigation if the result of litigation contains new information indicating misconduct.

3.15 Post-resignation investigations. Even if an employee resigns, consideration should be given to investigating the complaint as if the employee were still employed.

Commentary

The decision to complete the investigation of a complaint against an employee who has resigned is complex. The decision includes, but is not limited to, resources, local employment ordinances, interagency cooperation, agency self-critical analysis, and public confidence.

Resources

Continuing the investigation of a resigned employee could consume resources that might be needed elsewhere. Particularly if the investigation involves many witnesses, extensive travel, the resource-consuming retrieval or storage of evidence, the use of investigators who have other pressing cases to work on, or other situations taxing the agency's Internal Affairs resources, resources could be a legitimate factor in deciding whether to pursue a post-resignation case.

Local Employment Ordinances

The hiring/rehiring practices (including collective bargaining agreements) of many agencies are often determined by the ordinances of their local government. These may include rules requiring the rehire of previous employees unless there is documentation of reason to reject the rehire. "Reason to reject" standards can differ among jurisdictions, and an agency choosing not to complete the complaint investigation may be forced to rehire a bad employee because of it.

Interagency Cooperation

Because agencies often hire each other's personnel, a potential employer may end up hiring a bad employee for want of good information in the candidate's prior agency file. If an employee were to resign in lieu of termination and seek employment elsewhere, the agency he seeks to get hired by may not be able to determine his worthiness for hire if the agency he left did not finish the complaint investigation. If the practice of not completing investigations were widespread, agencies would find it more difficult to reject questionable prior-service applicants.

There are other means to determine whether an applicant has been a problem to a previous employer, and it is not necessarily the duty of one employer to protect potential employers from hiring mistakes. Yet as homeland security draws law enforcement into more sophisticated information-sharing relationships of all kinds, the question of how to document and share information related to the conditions in which an employee left an agency may become more important. It is not hard to imagine communities of agencies, particularly those likely to draw from the same employee pool, creating pacts or memoranda of agreement just for information on terminated or resigned employees. Such agreements could help prevent dangerous hiring errors, even a scenario in which a problem employee resigns upon accusation of passing unauthorized information only to find easy access to hiring at another agency.

In short, whether an agency completes a complaint investigation or not on an employee who has resigned, each agency should consider the benefit of developing local agreements to help determine the protocol for each agency's response to a resigned employee's complaint.

Agency Self-Critical Analysis

Information gained from a complaint can teach an agency about its policies, personnel, and activities that it may not learn otherwise. The careful leader will examine the complaint—wherever it is in the process when the employee resigns—for possible insights that might be gained if the complaint investigation were comprehensively done. An intuitive question such as, "What would make an employee feel like she could get away with this?" may lead to insights about the state of your field supervision or your agency's training. The answer to the question, "How did this supervisor harass this person for so long without anyone reporting it?" could lead to insight into the state of your discrimination enforcement practices. These kinds of questions do not require any more than common inquisitiveness and are well within the skill set of most agency managers.

Public Confidence

To complete the investigation reassures the public and agency employees that all complaints are taken seriously and provides the necessary safeguards to ensure a truthful outcome.

4.0 Mediation, Adjudication, and Disposition

Once a complaint investigation is completed, the agency has to determine what it will do with it. The agency also has to determine what it will do with the employee at the conclusion of the adjudication. This section explores the pathway and some of the most important considerations of that process.

Section Topics:

4.1   The four basic resolution categories.

4.2   The value of considering commanding officers' options.

4.3   Proposed reporting relationship of the head of Internal Affairs.

4.4   Standards for adjudication.

4.5   Penalty assessment and the use of a penalty matrix.

4.6   The advantages of mediation and the conditions of its use.

4.7   Settlement agreements and their value.

4.8   Exploring alternatives to traditional discipline.

4.9   Keeping investigations confidential.

4.10 Guidelines for selecting and retaining Internal Affairs investigators.

4.1 The four basic resolution categories. The findings in completed investigations should result in one of four resolutions: 1. sustained or founded; 2. not sustained or not resolved or unresolved; 3. exonerated; or 4. unfounded. Some unique state or local laws may require the addition of further categorical distinctions for some limited special circumstances.

Commentary

In general terms, a "founded" or "sustained" adjudication means that the allegations are true by a preponderance of the evidence and that the conduct at issue is a violation of agency rules. An "unfounded" adjudication means that the allegations are not true. A "not resolved" or "unresolved" or "not sustained" adjudication means that the allegations cannot be proven true or untrue by a preponderance of the evidence. "Exonerated" means that the conduct at issue occurred but is not a violation of agency rules.

Dispositions other than the basic four recommended above can be useful in categorizing outcomes that do not fall neatly into the basic four. One agency, for example, uses a disposition of "Actions Could Have Been Different" to depict a situation where the employee's actions were less than ideal but were not misconduct. The disposition includes check boxes to indicate what measures were taken to improve performance, including "Counseling," "Training," etc. While such a disposition has shown useful in the agency, it is based on that agency's broader disciplinary scheme, which may not apply to many others. Further, even that agency still also uses the basic four dispositions above.

Another reason to consider additional dispositions arises for agencies that use intelligent data systems to monitor employee conduct. The basic four dispositions are generally informative when assessing an employee's discipline history, but increasing the information resolution or granularity of a tracking or "early intervention" system's input can also improve the quality of decisions based on it. The more descriptive the dispositions, the more the decision-maker knows about the employee and the greater the decision space for the agency's leaders.

If an agency chooses to use case dispositions beyond the basic four, it should do so carefully, employing only those that have a clearly defined function in its personnel processes. This is particularly true for agencies with data-driven employee monitoring systems. When doing annual agency- or unit-wide analyses for trends, results are less useful if disposition categories change often because comparisons are not identically matched. Adding new disposition categories is like adding any other new field to a data system: it takes time to acquire enough events to produce a meaningful comparative dataset, and the smaller the number of new entries, the longer it often takes to derive meaning from them.

4.2 The value of considering commanding officers' options. The recommendations of commanding officers and their chain-of-command superiors regarding the adjudications of cases and the actions taken regarding the accused employees should be considered by the final deciding authority.

Commentary

Commanding officers have an important interest in administrative actions involving their employees. Commanding officers typically have more knowledge of their employees than does the agency head, including their histories and reputations in the unit, the employees' workplace environment, and sometimes their personal lives. Commanding officers have to continue cultivating their employees and their relationships with agency members and the public long after the cases conclude. The insights and interests of commanding officers could be important considerations in the determination of final case dispositions.

Involving commanding officers in the decision-making process can also be an opportunity for the agency head to mentor and develop the leadership and management acumen of their commanding officers, while in the same transactions learning from managers about conditions in the agency they might otherwise not know.

4.3 Proposed reporting relationship of the head of Internal Affairs. The head of Internal Affairs should preferably report directly to the agency head. If a direct reporting relationship is not feasible, the Internal Affairs commanding officer should nonetheless have prompt, unrestricted, and confidential access to all agency executives, including the agency head.

Commentary

For purposes of independence, confidentiality, direct and unfiltered discussion, and some freedom from institutional politics and pressures, the head of Internal Affairs should report directly to the agency head. The role of Internal Affairs is too vital to the integrity of the agency to risk message transmission errors, misinterpretations, or personal biases that would interfere with the agency head's clearest understanding of cases and their contexts.

4.4 Standards for adjudication. Adjudicators within the agency should use neutral and objective criteria, weigh evidence appropriately to distinguish strong evidence from questionable or less material evidence, and not indulge in presumptions that bias the findings of fact. The rationale for each adjudication should be in writing, and clearly related to the conduct, the employee, and the agency's rules.

Commentary

Minimum standards for adjudication of disciplinary cases include the following:

1. The burden of proof is on the agency.

2. The standard of proof is a preponderance of the evidence.

3. The standards of evidence are those of administrative law, not criminal law.

4. No presumptions of truth are made regarding facts in dispute.

5. No presumptions are made regarding witness credibility: all persons are equally credible unless an objective, fact-based evaluation of the witness's capacities, estimonial coherence, and other relevant and demonstrable factors justify otherwise.

6. Conclusions are logically deduced from the evidence.

A thorough review of adjudicative standards would exceed the scope of this report and would more easily be found in legal reference works or state jury instructions on assessing evidence and testimony. Nevertheless, an adjudication lacking in any of the six standards above should not be considered properly justified.

In weighing evidence, facts revealing a pattern of conduct should be considered. Where there is evidence that an employee has been accused of the same act before in other cases involving other independent complainants, the adjudicator may have reason to believe that the currently alleged act is not an isolated incident. Without contrary evidence, the greater the number of previous allegations of a substantially similar act, the more likely than not the current case is sustained.

Pattern of conduct evidence is evidence of specific acts, not merely categories of allegations. For example, if an officer has a history of complaints for rudeness, but each complainant alleges that the officer used different language, the pattern may be too general to be valuable. However, if in previous cases complainants alleged that the officer used a substantially similar offensive phrase or wording as used in the current case, the pattern may be specific enough to be valuable in considering a "sustained" finding.

Pattern of conduct evidence may come from complaints that were sustained or not resolved. However, unfounded complaints, where it was determined that the alleged act did not occur, are not suitable as pattern of conduct evidence.

Pattern of conduct evidence may also come from interviews of persons who had never been complainants. When investigating a rudeness allegation, for example, if the investigator were to contact persons to whom the officer had given traffic citations and found some who stated that the officer used the same rude phrase or wording with them, a pattern of conduct can be established.

Sometimes pattern of conduct is a consideration in the investigative phase depending on the model of investigation and adjudication the agency uses.

4.5 Penalty assessment and the use of a penalty matrix.

Agencies should have some system or mechanism to ensure that discipline is fair and consistent. A penalty matrix or similar schedule has proven helpful to some agencies whose disciplinary systems are based on a "progressive discipline" theory or collective bargaining agreement. In such systems a matrix can help ensure consistency, objectivity, and predictable penalties for misconduct. A matrix best involves recommended ranges of discipline, allowing for the decision-maker to consider the totality of the circumstances, including aggravating and mitigating factors, in determining appropriate discipline.

Commentary

A matrix specifies the nature of offenses or policy violations and associates them with specific penalty options or ranges of discipline. Within such a system, a policy violation falls within a certain class or category of violation that, in turn, corresponds to a particular range or set of discipline options that a decision-maker can consider according to the totality of the circumstances present in a given case.

A matrix is a helpful tool but should not be applied inflexibly. The decision-maker should consider the totality of the circumstances, aggravating and mitigating factors, nondisciplinary outcomes, precedent, and consistency. Precedent, in the sense of prior disciplinary decisions for the same conduct, should be considered but should not straitjacket the decision-maker. As times and police culture change, as the acuteness of particular forms of misconduct may grow in the eyes of the agency or the public, so also must disciplinary decisions change to reflect contemporary ethics and judgments about police behavior. While discipline should be reasonably predictable, fair punishment reflective of current ethical standards should not be held hostage to what may have been done in the past.

Broad disciplinary categories, such as Conduct Unbecoming an Officer, may be useful, but in order to give the greatest value to a matrix, it is suggested that misconduct be described more precisely.

4.6 The advantages of mediation and the conditions of its use. Voluntary mediation conducted by a neutral facilitator, in lieu of investigation and adjudication, permits resolution of minor complaints that are usually not easily resolved through investigation. Mediation should be encouraged except where an officer has a pattern of similar misconduct or where a broader review of the employee's performance suggests a need to analyze the results of the investigation in the current case. Agencies should consider enacting policies to codify all aspects of their mediation procedures.

Commentary

Mediation engages the community by giving individual members of the public who make a complaint the opportunity to have their concerns heard and considered in a way that might not otherwise occur if the complaint was investigated and adjudicated through the formal Internal Affairs process. Mediation is best used as a means of allowing an officer and a citizen to better understand each other's perspectives. Mediation should not take place unless the complainant and the subject officer each voluntarily agreed to mediate.

Complaints best resolved through mediation are complaints of officer discourtesy or rudeness and others that involve minor "one-on-one" interactions between officers and members of the community. The types of complaints that can be mediated should be described in a clear written policy. The determination whether a given complaint is eligible for mediation should be made according to guidelines established by the agency, including the rank or positions authorized to permit mediation.

Some agencies offer an incentive to officers who agreed to mediate. All agencies should establish written policies to ensure that an officer cannot elect to mediate multiple complaints where there is the possibility of a pattern or practice of misconduct or a motive to circumvent discipline or otherwise bypass an agency's early intervention system.

The decision to use internal or external facilitators may vary from agency to agency. Outside facilitators may make community members more comfortable that the mediation process is not biased against them or toward the officer, in turn making mediation a more attractive option, as well as a more effective means of improving relations with the community. Mediations facilitated by a member of the agency provide an opportunity for the agency's leaders to learn more about the conduct and attitudes of their employees. Above all, the person chosen to mediate the dispute must be adequately trained in dispute resolution and strive to mediate in a neutral and objective manner.

4.7 Settlement agreements and their value. Well-reasoned and fully justified settlement agreements, conditional suspensions of discipline, "last-chance" agreements, and legitimate dropping of charges or mitigation of penalties should be available when to do so will not undermine the values of fairness, consistency, predictability, and integrity. Decisions to modify discipline should be justified in writing.

Commentary

While it is important and efficient to settle grievances to avoid a proliferation of appeals and reviews, it is more important that individual officers or their representatives not be able to manipulate the system. Untrammeled deal making and plea bargaining can make a disciplinary system arbitrary, unpredictable, and introduce luck into the final disciplinary determination. In a thorough investigation, each founded charge against an officer will be supported by sufficient proof such that an impartial and honest reviewer will be hard-pressed to overturn a disciplinary decision.

There is a place nonetheless for settlement and last-chance agreements and mitigation in appropriate circumstances. Some agencies hold penalties in full or partial abeyance and do not make the officer serve the actual numbers of days off if the officer's conduct in the next year is free of similar misconduct. Wisely deployed, these devices can be a useful and progressive way to encourage good behavior. Used unwisely, habitual suspension of sentences can encourage excessive deal making and introduce arbitrariness into the disciplinary system.

4.8 Exploring alternatives to traditional discipline.

Creative alternatives to traditional punitive discipline may be useful in improving the performance of wayward employees in ways traditional punitive discipline is not. This is an area typically unexplored in larger agencies until recently and warrants further research and development.

Commentary

Traditional punitive discipline operates under a theory akin to criminal justice: an offense is committed and a punishment is imposed as a response. Typically in the interests of fairness, consistency, "progressive discipline," and to deter further misconduct, the punishment imposed attempts to match the seriousness of the offense and the history of the offender. According to this theory, a corollary benefit of deterring the misconduct of the general employee population arises as those who have not yet committed misconduct see the punishment of those who have. The basis for this traditional model is the presumption that punishment either initially deters misconduct or succeeds at changing the behavior of recipients of punishment who were not initially deterred. Law enforcement agencies should be encouraged to explore nondisciplinary resolutions where other and more powerful means exist to change or modify conduct.

One alternative model is being developed[3] in which the employer's response to employee transgressions is not to seek a penalty to fit the offense, but to find a strategy to fit the employee.[4] One phrase used to help inculcate this model is, "Think first strategy, not penalty."

According to this strategic model, in cases where core facts are not at issue in a sustained complaint, a particular interactive process helps determine the error in thinking that led the employee to commit the problem act. The identification of the problem thinking provides the leader with a starting point from which to determine what strategy is likely to (a) reveal the errant thinking to the employee, (b) lead the employee to come up with a solution to change the errant thinking, and (c) enable the employee to transfer the new thinking to all situations in which the relevant principles—not just the rules—apply. Leading the employee to recognize the principles is a crucial feature of the system.

---

[3]This model is being developed and implemented by Los Angeles Police Department Deputy Chief Mark R. Perez, the commanding officer of LAPD's Professional Standards Bureau.

[4]This applies only to nondischarge cases: employees whose acts render them unfit for duty are discharged from employment according to civil service rules. Such employees are beyond the reach of employee development.

The question of "penalty" is not important if the focus is on what is most likely to reinforce the employee's new understanding of the principles and his obligations within them. A suspension or other punitive action is not necessarily the best way to induce improved thinking and behavior for most employees. For the strategic model, the presumption is that behavior changes by influencing the employee's thinking toward acting on explicit principles, not just rules.

Another system is being developed[5] in which alternatives to traditional discipline are pursued that are more constructive than punitive. An existing collective bargaining agreement already permits officers to surrender vacation days in lieu of being suspended. This is referred to in the contract as "Positive Discipline." The agency, however, is seeking to go beyond "Positive Discipline" by creatively finding nonpunitive means to train, remediate, or otherwise involve officers in constructive activities to reorient their conduct. One constructive alternative, for example, is offering an officer the opportunity to participate in community projects within the jurisdiction, like doing free home repairs for persons who could not otherwise afford the labor costs in the open market. While an officer could decline the offer for the alternative activity, the system is nevertheless designed to increase the number of ways employees' actions can be reoriented to the agency's standards.

Both the strategic model and the constructive alternatives model share the following understandings:

1. The adverse effects of the traditional punishment model are considerable:

   a. Punishment forces the employee to suffer loss, but does not reveal or necessarily resolve the underlying problem motivating the misconduct.

   b. Punishment, especially in the form of unpaid suspensions, harms more than just the employee: the employee's family loses money, the agency loses a deployment asset, and the jurisdiction's citizens lose the safety work the employee would have provided had he not been suspended.

---

[5]This system is being developed and implemented in the Houston Police Department under the direction of Deputy Chief Michael Dirden.

c. Punishment can create bitterness rather than a desire to improve.

d. Punishment can contribute to a code of silence—an unwillingness of employees to admit to or report misconduct—if the punishment is seen as costly.

e. The threat of punishment for misconduct can deter employees from engaging in desirable self-initiated activities if the discipline system is seen to punish rule violations mechanically or captiously rather than reasonably.

f. Punishment creates a constant threat of legal and labor actions against the employer that often takes significant resources to manage.

2. Properly done, alternative systems can have significant advantages over employee punishment:

a. The adverse effects of punishment either disappear or minimize when punishment disappears or is minimized.

b. Alternative systems often find the causes of the problems of the misconduct and resolve them at their root.

c. Alternative systems tend to inspire goodwill in employees toward their work, their employer, and their agency's constituents

d. Alternative systems help create organizations where employees learn their responsibilities through direct mentoring interactions with their leaders and mutually-crafted development plans

e. Alternative systems impose and clarify a burden of responsibility on the employee to improve, not to suffer. Punitive systems impose only the burden of suffering a penalty.

f. Alternative systems make it easier to identify employees to be discharged: an employee who, after having had the opportunity to help reorient his thinking and actions based on an understanding of the agency's principles still violates those principles can no longer be seen as merely ignorant of those principles. Misconduct, especially a repeated violation of principles well conveyed in earlier employee development sessions, then becomes strong evidence of the employee's refusal to adopt the agency's standards. Alternative systems clarify the employee's intent far more clearly than the typical incrementally increasing "progressive discipline" of traditional punitive systems. Alternative systems can let the employer know a lot sooner when a recalcitrant employee should be terminated.

There are many more features and advantages to the strategic model and the constructive alternatives model than can be explained here. The point, however, is not to exhaustively detail the systems in this report, but to acknowledge that there are means other than traditional punitive discipline being seriously explored in the Internal Affairs community of practice, and that this is an area worthy of serious research and development.

4.9 Keeping investigations confidential. Internal affairs investigations should be closed to the officer and the public during their pendency. Nonetheless, the agency head should be fully informed of the progress of internal investigations and should regularly communicate the status of an investigation to the press and general public to the full extent permitted by law.

Commentary

To ensure that an officer's rights are preserved during the course of an Internal Affairs investigation, and to minimize interference and undue pressure on Internal Affairs and the department at large, it is important that investigations remain confidential during their pendency. There is nonetheless an obligation to keep the public informed of the progress of an investigation and such other disclosures that can be made without compromising the investigation and to the extent allowed by law.

4.10 Guidelines for selecting and retaining Internal Affairs investigators. To make certain that Internal Affairs units benefit from high-quality and experienced employees, agencies should consider utilizing promotional policies that recognize service in Internal Affairs as productive and useful for advancing an officer's career, and they should make such policies explicit and well-publicized. Tours in Internal Affairs should be limited to fixed terms.

Commentary

Agencies should consider providing officers with incentives to work in Internal Affairs, such as an explicit policy that places service in that unit as highly advantageous for promotional or assignment purposes.

Specific requirements should be established for the selection of individuals to work in Internal Affairs. Prior investigative experience or a strong investigative background should either serve as a requirement or a significant qualification for Internal Affairs service. Consideration should also be given to using supervisors instead of nonsupervisors because supervisors typically have agency-wide interests and accountability, and are likely to consider broader organizational questions beyond just the question of guilt or innocence in the instant case.

Selected candidates should sign a confidentiality agreement that clearly states that it is an act of misconduct for an Internal Affairs investigator to reveal investigative information to any person, regardless of rank, unless that person has an authorized right and need to know, whether that revelation is made during or after the investigator's tour of duty in Internal Affairs.

After being selected, the agency should provide as much ongoing training or professional development in investigation and Internal Affairs investigation as possible, including training in effective interview techniques, development of case strategy, laws that apply to Internal Affairs investigations, and other subjects relevant to fulfilling the investigative mission.

Consideration should be given to limiting the tour of duty in Internal Affairs. One agency limits its tours to 2 or 3 years, with two 1-year extensions permitted in unusual circumstances up to a maximum of 5 years. There are at least several reasons for limiting the tour of service. Too long a stay in Internal Affairs may, in some cases, create investigators who become biased. The development of such an attitude—or any other bias—is not helpful to the employee or the investigations. In some cases, investigators become emotionally drained or even bored after extended stays in Internal Affairs. It is a uniquely difficult assignment and its psychological effects are important in determining whether a tour limit should apply and how long it might be.

The experience in Internal Affairs can be extremely valuable in the promotion process and in giving promotees a view on employee behavior that would not be available elsewhere. Seeing firsthand the kinds of trouble people get into by investigating the incidents and talking with the persons harmed by the allegations and the misconduct is a management insight that should be offered to as many qualified people as is practical. Also, knowing that not all allegations are true—even the most horrific ones—helps those who leave Internal Affairs respond correctly to allegations that come before them as they advance in rank. Finally, there is a wisdom that comes from dealing with the complexities of investigative controversies from start to finish that can be invaluable in helping form a mature leader. Allowing as many qualified investigators as practical to acquire that wisdom by cycling them through Internal Affairs can infuse the agency with a maturity in the leadership team they may otherwise lack.

Appendix: A Sampling of Major City Police Force Discipline Policies

On May 5, 2005, The Los Angeles Police Department was awarded a grant by the U.S. Department of Justice Office of Community Oriented Policing Services to convene and coordinate a National Internal Affairs Community of Practice comprising 12 major city and county police agencies. The Community of Practice's goal was to develop standards and best practices in Internal Affairs work and to share this work with the wider law enforcement community.

The Community of Practice soon discovered that there were significant differences among the participating agencies. In an effort to focus the discussion and ensure the development of a workable set of guidelines, Merrick Bobb, President, Police Assessment Resource Center, developed a matrix that would provide a snapshot of each agency's current policies and structures in the key areas of Internal Affairs: intake, classification, investigation, recommendation, adjudication, and discipline. Input from other agencies not directly participating in the Community of Practice was also sought.

We hope the matrices will provide a basic understanding of the organization and policies of the contributing police agencies and help guide policy development and organizational structure for the wider law enforcement community.

Internal Affairs Matrix—Atlanta Police Department

Intake

Manner in which complaints can be received: Any Source

Anonymous complaints accepted: (Y)

Third-party complaints accepted: (Y)

Penalty of perjury for false statements: (Y Officers)

Dispose of complaint prior to classification: (Y)

If Y, how? Supervisor on-scene, but if complainant insists complaint must be taken.

Complaint forms numbered and tracked: (Y)

Complaint is forwarded for classification to: Office of Professional Standards

Classification

A complaint can be classified as: Maltreatment or Unnecessary Force, Vehicle Accident, Sexual Misconduct, Standard Operating Procedure, Property/Evidence, Person Shot, Misc., Firearms Discharge, FTA, Criminal Domestic, Criminal, Courtesy, Attendance.

Once classified, a complaint is assigned to: Sergeant or Investigator

Investigation

At what command level is each type of complaint investigated: The Office of Professional Standards Investigates Priority I Complaints; Employee's Supervisor Investigates Priority II Complaints

Investigation is supervised/reviewed by:

In OPS Lieutenant

Priority II Employee's Supervisor

Recommendation

IA recommends findings (sustained, not sustained, etc.): (Y)

If Y, who makes recommendation:

IA Commander- Lieutenant

The recommendation is made to:

OPS Commander - Major

If Y, who reviews recommendation:

If Sustained, E's Chain of command;

If Not Sustained, No further Review

Adjudication

IA makes findings (sustained, not sustained, etc.): (Y)

Complaints go back through the Chain of Command for adjudication: (Y)

If Y, who makes final disposition:

Chief of Police or His Designee

Categories of findings: Sustained, Not Sustained, Exonerated, Unfounded, Exceptionally Closed

Discipline

IA recommends discipline: (N)

If Y, who makes recommendation:

The recommendation is made to:

Chief of Police or His Designee

Discipline is ultimately imposed by:

Chief of Police or His Designee

IA is under what division/office: The Office of the Chief

IA is headed by: Lieutenant

Head of IA reports to: Major

Rank of IA investigators: Investigators and Sergeants

Number of IA investigators: 24

Total number of sworn employees: 1,786

Internal Affairs Matrix—Boston Police Department

Intake

Manner in which complaints can be received:
Any method of complaint is processed
Anonymous complaints accepted: yes
Third-party complaints accepted: yes
Penalty of perjury for false statements: no
Dispose of complaint prior to classification: yes
When the allegation of misconduct does not describe a violation of our rules, the receiving superior officer will document it and forward to C.O. then to IAD Commander.

Classification

A complaint can be classified as: Violation of Rules/Procedures-with the allegation specifying the conduct. Misconduct of any kind will be included in our rules.

Once classified, a complaint is assigned to: Investig. Sgt. Det. or Lt. Det.

Investigation

At what command level is each type of complaint investigated: Sgt. Det. or Lt. Det. will investigate all allegations of misconduct.

Investigation is supervised/reviewed by:
Lt. Det. and Deputy Superin.

Recommendation

IA recommends findings (sustained, not sustained, etc.): yes
If Y, who makes recommendation: Investigator, IAD Commander, Bureau Chief, and Legal Advisor reviews
The recommendation is made to: Up chain of command to P. Commissioner
Recommendations reviewed at each level

If Y, who reviews recommendation:

Adjudication

IA makes findings (sustained, not sustained, etc.): No
Complaints go back through the Chain of Command for adjudication: No, complaints go up chain, not down chain.
If Y, who makes final disposition: Up chain of command to P.C.. P.C. makes final disposition.

Categories of findings: Sustained, Not Sustained, Exonerated, Unfounded

Discipline

IA recommends discipline: No
If Y, who makes recommendation: Bureau Chief, Assist Bureau Chief, Legal advisor jointly recommend to P. Commissioner.

The recommendation is made to: PC

Discipline is ultimately imposed by: PC

IA is under what division/office: Bureau of Internal Investigation
IA is headed by: Deputy Superintendent
Head of IA reports to: Superintendent Bureau Internal Investigations
Rank of IA investigators: Sgt. Det. and Lt. Det.
Number of IA investigators: Twelve: Nine Sg. Dets. report to three Lt. Dets. – three teams
Total number of sworn employees: 2,050

Internal Affairs Matrix—Chicago Police Department

Intake

Manner in which complaints can be received: In person, police facility or OPS, via phone, via letter, via tty. web-based under development

Anonymous complaints accepted: (Y) Limited to criminal, residency and medical abuse

Third-party complaints accepted: (Y)

Penalty of perjury for false statements: (Y) under state law (never utilized – law is only 18 mos. old).

Dispose of complaint prior to classification: (N) Classification occurs prior save for those complaints in which no misconduct occurs

Classification

A complaint can be classified as: Variety. First determined if use of force or other. Civilians investigate use of force at OPS. IAD gets all else, results in myriad classifications, 15 categories in all

Once classified, a complaint is assigned to: After force decision, then generally facts determine where assigned. Serious corruption, criminal, residency, medical integrity, bias, EEO, civil suits and Lts and above always go to IAD. Rest may go to field or IAD

Investigation

At what command level is each type of complaint investigated: Field – sergeants or rank above accused. IAD – officers, police agents and sergeants conduct all investigations. OPS – civilian

Investigation is supervised/reviewed by:
Field – watch commander to exempt district commander through at least 2 levels of chain. IAD – IAD Unit CO (Lt) and through field chain, at least 2 levels.

Recommendation

IA recommends findings (sustained, not sustained, etc.): (Y)

If Y, who makes recommendation:
Field - Supervisor, IAD any rank.

The recommendation is made to: Superintendent (Chief)

If Y, who reviews recommendation: Each level of chain of the accused for a minimum of two levels of review. Can recommend alternate finding or further investigation, cannot require. Only the Superintendent can change finding.

Adjudication

IA makes findings (sustained, not sustained, etc.): (Y) Complaints go back through the Chain of Command for adjudication: (N) No, review only. Alternate recommendation can be made.

If Y, who makes final disposition: Superintendent makes final recommendation. ADS IAD is responsible for identifying and evaluating input of chain

Categories of findings: Sustained, Not Sustained, Unfounded, Exonerated, Non-cooperation.

Discipline

IA recommends discipline: (Y)

If Y, who makes recommendation: Supervisor assigned to investigator, if other than sergeant.

The recommendation is made to: Superintendent

Discipline is ultimately imposed by: Superintendent, with review by police board of suspensions more than 6 days. Separation is sole decision of Police Board, Supt. only recommends separation.

IA is under what division/office: Office of the Superintendent, direct reporting

IA is headed by: Assistant Deputy Superintendent

Head of IA reports to: Superintendent

Rank of IA investigators: Sergeant, Detective, Police Agent, Police Officer

Number of IA investigators: 74

Total number of sworn employees: 13, 600

Internal Affairs Matrix—Dallas Police Department

Intake

Manner in which complaints can be received: IAD Walk-ins, Signed fax, Internal Request for Control Number (signed form), Station walk-ins— verbally refer complainant to IAD w/station supervisor completing written FYI to IAD.

Anonymous complaints accepted: (N)

Third-party complaints accepted: (N)

Penalty for perjury for false statements: (very rare)

Dispose of complaint prior to classification: (Y)

If Y, how? Mediation,

Complaint forms numbered and tracked: (Y)

Complaint is forwarded for classification to: Informal IAD Committee

Classification

A complaint can be classified as: (1)IAD-Investigation is conducted by IAD detective. (2)Division Referral-Complaint is referred to the accused employee's division for a supervisor to investigate. (3)Mediation-Process is overseen by mediation sergeant. (4)Public Integrity Unit—Criminal allegations investigated by PIU detective.

Once classified, a complaint is assigned to:

See above explanation

Investigation

At what command level is each type of complaint investigated: IAD- Detectives conduct all unless very high profile, or high-ranking officer accused, then conducted by sergeant. Seldom a lieutenant. Mediation—Sergeant.

Division Referral–Sergeant.

Public Integrity Unit–Mirrors IAD.

Investigation is supervised/reviewed by:
(1) Sergeant (2) Lieutenant
(3) Deputy Chief/IAD Commander

Recommendation

IA recommends findings (sustained, not sustained, etc.): (Y)

If Y, who makes recommendation: Originally, the investigating detective, with review and concurrence through Deputy Chief if sustained. If not sustained, reviewed with concurrence through lieutenant.

The recommendation is made to:

Chief of Police

If Y, who reviews recommendation: Ultimately C.o.P. on sustained. IAD Lt. On others.

Adjudication

IA makes findings (sustained, not sustained, etc.): (Y)

Complaints go back through the Chain of Command for adjudication: (Y)

If Y, who makes final disposition: IAD makes final disposition, of course C.o.P. can overturn IAD. Categories of findings: Sustained, Inconclusive, Unfounded, Exonerated, Complete

Discipline

IA recommends discipline: (N)

If Y, who makes recommendation: Each level of accused employee's chain of command makes discipline recommendation.

The recommendation is made to:

Chief of Police

Discipline is ultimately imposed by:
Chief of Police

IA is under what division/office: Administrative & Support Bureau

IA is headed by: Deputy Chief Calvin Cunigan

Head of IA reports to: Bureau Commander- Assistant Chief Tom Ward

Rank of IA investigators: Senior Corporal

Number of IA investigators: 24

Total number of sworn employees: 3,043

Internal Affairs Matrix—Detroit Police Department

Intake

Manner in which complaints can be received: In person, telephonically, written, e-mail, anonymously,

Anonymous complaints accepted: (Y)

Third-party complaints accepted: (Y)

Penalty of perjury for false statements: (Y)

Dispose of complaint prior to classification: (Y)

If Y, how?

Conducting a preliminary investigation

Complaint forms numbered and tracked: (Y)

Complaint is forwarded for classification to: Commanding Officer of Internal Affairs

Classification

A complaint can be classified as: Criminal, Serious Departmental Misconduct that will be investigated by Internal Affairs or referred back to the Office of the Chief Investigator or the involved officer's command for investigation

Once classified, a complaint is assigned to: Internal Affairs, Involved Officer's Command, Office of the Chief Investigator (Civilian Revue)

Investigation

At what command level is each type of complaint investigated: Criminal allegations and Serious Departmental Misconduct–Internal Affairs

Demeanor, Procedure, Search, Service– Office of the Chief Investigator (Civilian Revue)

Minor Departmental Misconduct– Involved Officer's Command

Investigation is supervised/reviewed by:

C.O. IA, C.O. OCI, C.O. Inv. Ofc.'s Command

Recommendation

IA recommends findings (sustained, not sustained, etc.): (Y)

If Y, who makes recommendation: Officer in Charge of the case. Internal Affairs

The recommendation is made to: Disciplinary Administration

If Y, who reviews recommendation: C.O. Internal Affairs

Adjudication

IA makes findings (sustained, not sustained, etc.): (Y)

Complaints go back through the Chain of Command for adjudication: (Y)

If Y, who makes final disposition: Commanding Officer's Hearing, Trial Board (Dep. Chief & two Cmdrs.), Chief, Arbitrator

Categories of findings: Guilty, Not Guilty, Dismissed

Discipline

IA recommends discipline: (Y)

If Y, who makes recommendation: C.O. Internal Affairs

The recommendation is made to: Disciplinary Administration Unit

Discipline is ultimately imposed by: Trial Board (Dep. Chief & two Cmdrs.), Chief, Arbitrator

IA is under what division/office: Office of the Chief of Police

IA is headed by: Commander

Head of IA reports to: Chief of Police

Rank of IA investigators: Sergeants and Lieutenants

Number of IA investigators: Approximately 20

Total number of sworn employees: Approximately 3,700

Internal Affairs Matrix—Houston Police Department

Intake

Manner in which complaints can be received: anonymous, in person, fax, letter, telephone.

Anonymous complaints accepted: (Yes)

Third-party complaints accepted: (Yes)

Penalty of perjury for false statements: (Yes)

Dispose of complaint prior to classification: (Yes)

If Y, how?

Modified as Duplicate, or CIO Issue.

Complaint forms numbered and tracked: (Yes)

Complaint is forwarded for classification to: Central Intake Office

Classification

A complaint can be classified as:

Class I – Criminal Allegations

Class II – Policy Violations

Once classified, a complaint is assigned to: Class I to Internal Affairs Division. Class II to Division Concerned.

Investigation

At what command level is each type of complaint investigated: Sergeants are assigned to investigate complaints.

Investigation is supervised/reviewed by: Lieutenants.

Recommendation

IA recommends findings (sustained, not sustained, etc.): (Yes)

If Y, who makes recommendation: Lieutenant who supervised the investigation and writes the investigative synopsis.

The recommendation is made to: Chief of Police

If Y, who reviews recommendation: Captain, Assistant Chief and Chief of Police.

Adjudication

IA makes findings (sustained, not sustained, etc.): (Yes)

Complaints go back through the Chain of Command for adjudication: (Yes)

If Y, who makes final disposition: Chief of Police

Categories of findings:

Sustained, Not Sustained, Unfounded, Exonerated

Discipline

IA recommends discipline: (No)

If Y, who makes recommendation: Employee's Captain makes recommendation Reviewed by Assistant Chief and Administrative Disciplinary Committee.

The recommendation is made to: Chief of Police

Discipline is ultimately imposed by: Chief of Police

IA is under what division/office: Internal Investigations Command

IA is headed by: Captain of Police

Head of IA reports to: Assistant Chief, Internal Investigations Command

Rank of IA investigators: Sergeant

Number of IA investigators: 26 (Includes Reactive and Proactive investigators)

Total number of sworn employees: 4,781

Internal Affairs Matrix—Los Angeles Police Department

Intake

Manner in which complaints can be received:
In person; telephonic; e-mail; TDD; verbal; written (complaint form or any other); by any means.

Anonymous complaints accepted: (Y)

Third-party complaints accepted: (Y)

Penalty of perjury for false statements: (N)

Dispose of complaint prior to classification: (N)
If Y, how?

Complaint forms numbered and tracked: (Y)
Complaint is forwarded for classification to:
"Classifications Unit" specifically to classify

Classification

A complaint can be classified as: Any one or combination of 31 total classifications (see Page 2)

Once classified, a complaint is assigned to:
1. IA – Administrative
2. IA – Criminal
3. Chain of Command

Investigation

At what command level is each type of complaint investigated: Normally, Consent Decree paragraph 93 dictates where the case is assigned (see page 2), either IA or Chain of Command. We have a "Quick Team" at IA to handle those cases that have very minimum follow up potential, or clearly Demonstrably False.

Investigation is supervised/reviewed by: Officer in Charge (LT) or Commanding Ofcr (CAPT)

Recommendation

IA recommends findings (sustained, not sustained, etc.): (N)

If Y, who makes recommendation:

The recommendation is made to:

If Y, who reviews recommendation:

Adjudication

IA makes findings (sustained, not sustained, etc.): (N)
Complaints go back through the Chain of Command for adjudication: (Y)
If Y, who makes final disposition: Chief of Police

Categories of findings: (see Page 3)

Discipline

IA recommends discipline: (N)
If Y, who makes recommendation:

The recommendation is made to:

Discipline is ultimately imposed by: Chief of Police

IA is under what division/office: Professional Standards Bureau

IA is headed by: Commander

Head of IA reports to: Professional Standards Bureau C/O, who reports directly to Chief of Police

Rank of IA investigators: Sergeants II, and Detectives II

Number of IA investigators: 264

Total number of sworn employees: 9,734

Los Angeles Police Department

Classifications (31)

Alcohol Related	Unbecoming Conduct	Narcotics/Drugs
Domestic Violence	Off-Duty Altercation	Shooting Violation
Accidental Discharge	Improper Remark	Ethnic Remark
Discourtesy	Unauthorized Force	Unauthorized Tactics
Discrimination	Dishonesty	Insubordination
Theft	Neglect of Duty	Sexual Misconduct
Gender Bias	Unlawful Search	False Imprisonment
Other Policy/Rule	Failure to Appear	Failure to Qualify
Preventable Traffic Collision	Service	False Statements
Failure to Report Misconduct	Misleading Statements	Retaliation
Racial Profiling		

Consent Decree Paragraph 93

The following types of complaints shall be investigated by Internal Affairs Group:

All civil suits or claim for damages involved on-duty conduct by LAPD officers, or off duty where the employee's actions are tied to the LAPD.

Unauthorized uses of force

Invidious discrimination, including improper ethnic remarks and gender bias

Unlawful search

Unlawful seizure (including false arrest and false imprisonment)

Dishonesty

Domestic Violence

Narcotics/Drugs

Sexual Misconduct

Theft

Retaliation or retribution against an officer or civilian

- All incidents where 1) a civilian is charged by an officer with interfering with a police officer (Penal Code Section 148), resisting arrest, or disorderly conduct, *and 2*) the prosecutor's office notified the Department either that it is dismissing the charge based upon officer credibility, or a judge dismissed the charge based upon officer credibility.

- All incidents in which the Department has received written notification from a prosecuting agency in a criminal case that there has been an order suppressing evidence because of any constitutional violation involving potential misconduct by an LAPD officer; any other judicial finding of officer misconduct made in the course of a judicial proceeding; or any request by a federal or state judge or magistrate that a misconduct investigation be initiated puruant to some information developed during a judicial proceeding before a judge or magistrate.

(Los Angeles Police Department, continued)

- All incidents in which an officer is arrested or charged with a crime other than low grade misdemeanors.

- Any request by a judge or prosecutor that a misconduct investigation be initiated pursuant to information developed during the course of an official proceeding in which such judge or prosecutor has been involved.

Categories of Findings

Disciplinary:	Nondisciplinary:
Unfounded	Policy/Procedure
Not Resolved	Employee's Act Did Not Rise to the Level of Misconduct
Exonerated	Employee's Actions Could Have Been Different
Sustained – No Penalty	Training
Sustained – Penalty	Counseling
Admonishment	Comment Card
Official Reprimand	Notice to Correct Deficiencies
Suspension Days	Referral
Board of Rights	Demonstrably False
Demotion	Department Employee Not Involved
	Resolved through Alternative Complaint Resolution

Duplicate

Withdrawn by the Chief of Police

Insufficient Evidence to Adjudicate Complaint

Other Judicial Review

Internal Affairs Matrix—Los Angeles County Sheriff's Department

Intake

Manner in which PUBLIC complaints can be received:
Mail; e-mail; phone; in person; web site; fax;
1-800 complaint line

Anonymous complaints accepted: Yes
Third-party complaints accepted: Yes
Penalty of perjury for false statements: No
Dispose of complaint prior to classification: No
Complaint forms numbered and tracked: Yes
Complaint is forwarded for classification to:
Complaint is classified at intake

Classification

A complaint can be classified as:
Personnel or Service; personnel complaints can contain criminal or policy allegations. Policy allegations can be resolved by conducting a review, or by conducting an administrative investigation. Criminal allegations are investigated by the Internal Criminal Investigations Bureau (ICIB).
Once classified, a complaint is assigned to: It could be assigned to the employee's Unit, Internal Affairs, or ICIB.

Investigation

At what command level is each type of complaint investigated: Reviews are conducted by sergeants or lieutenants; unit-level administrative investigations are conducted by lieutenants; IA investigations are conducted by sergeants; criminal investigations are conducted by sergeants.
Investigation is supervised/reviewed by: Lieutenant; Captain; Commander; Chief

Recommendation

IA recommends findings (sustained, not sustained, etc.): No
If Y, who makes recommendation:

The recommendation is made to:

If Y, who reviews recommendation:

Adjudication

IA makes findings (sustained, not sustained, etc.): No
Complaints go back through the Chain of Command for adjudication: Yes
If Y, who makes final disposition: Captain and Chief for written rep to 15 days' suspension; Assistant Sheriffs and Undersheriff for 16-30 days' suspension, demotion, and discharge.

Categories of findings: Founded; Unresolved; Unfounded; Exonerated (for admin invest.)

Discipline

IA recommends discipline: No
If Y, who makes recommendation:

The recommendation is made to:

Discipline is ultimately imposed by: Employee's Unit Commander; Undersheriff (for discharge and demotion)

IA is under what division/office: Leadership and Training Division
IA is headed by: Captain
Head of IA reports to: Commander
Rank of IA investigators: Sergeant
Number of IA investigators: 22 (29 budgeted)
Total number of sworn employees: 8,346 (9,385 budgeted)

Internal Affairs Matrix—Metropolitan Police Department (Washington, D.C.)

Intake

Manner in which complaints can be received:

Anonymous complaints accepted: (Y)

Third-party complaints accepted: (Y)

Penalty of perjury for false statements: (Y)

Dispose of complaint prior to classification: (Y)

If Y, how?

Only in cases involving duplicate complaints.

Complaint forms numbered and tracked: (Y)

Complaint is forwarded for classification to: Director IAD for triage and classification change.

Classification

A complaint can be classified as:
- Administrative misconduct
- Criminal misconduct

Once classified, a complaint is assigned to:

Either IAD intake case or out to chain of command.

Investigation

At what command level is each type of complaint investigated:

Chain of command by members' supervisor

IAD intake by IAD agent or lieutenant if involving senior command official.

Investigation is supervised/reviewed by:

Supervised by IAD team lieutenant and reviewed by IAD captain and director.

Recommendation

IA recommends findings (sustained, not sustained, etc.): (Y)

If Y, who makes recommendation: The investigating IAD agent. Lt. or Capt. can "write over" if they do not concur with findings.

The recommendation is made to: thru director of IAD to Assistant Chief, Office of Prof. Responsibility.

Adjudication

IA makes findings (sustained, not sustained, etc.): Y

Complaints go back through the Chain of Command for adjudication: (Y) depending on severity.

If Y, who makes final disposition: Either involved member's C/O or Dept. Disciplinary Review Officer.

Categories of findings: Sustained, Insuff. Facts, Exonerated, Unfounded.

Discipline

IA recommends discipline: (Y)

If Y, who makes recommendation: The investigating IA agent

The recommendation is made to: Same as adjudication

Discipline is ultimately imposed by: Either member's C/O or Agency DDRO.

IA is under what division/office: Office of Professional Responsibility – Assistant Chief – direct report to Chief of Police.

IA is headed by: Rank of Inspector (one grade above Captain).

Head of IA reports to: Assistant Chief of OPR.

Rank of IA investigators: Detectives and Sergeants. Sergeants have no supervisory role.

Number of IA investigators: 30 for corruption/misconduct and 20 for serious uses of force (shootings, etc.)

Total number of sworn employees: 3,800

Internal Affairs Matrix—Miami-Dade Police Department

Intake

Manner in which complaints can be received: In person, telephone, mail, e-mail

Anonymous complaints accepted: (Y or N)

Third-party complaints accepted: (Y or N)

Penalty of perjury for false statements: (Y or N)

Dispose of complaint prior to classification: (Y or N)

If Y, how?

Complaint forms numbered and tracked: (Y or N)

Complaint is forwarded for classification to: Investigative sergeants

Classification

A complaint can be classified as: See Miami-Dade IA Matrix (2 of 2)

Once classified, a complaint is assigned to: Investigator (Sgt.)

Investigation

At what command level is each type of complaint investigated: A sergeant (first-line supervisor)

Investigation is supervised/reviewed by: Supervised by a Lieutenant/Reviewed by a Captain/Major

Recommendation

IA recommends findings (sustained, not sustained, etc.): (Y or N)

If Y, who makes recommendation:

The recommendation is made to:

If Y, who reviews recommendation:

Adjudication

IA makes findings (sustained, not sustained, etc.): (Y or N)

Complaints go back through the Chain of Command for adjudication: (Y or N)

If Y, who makes final disposition:

Categories of findings:

Discipline

IA recommends discipline: (Y or N)

If Y, who makes recommendation:

The recommendation is made to:

Discipline is ultimately imposed by: The Commander of the subject employee

---

IA is under what division/office: The Special Services Division

IA is headed by: A police major

Head of IA reports to: The Chief of the Special Services Division

Rank of IA investigators: Sergeant

Number of IA investigators: 35

Total number of sworn employees: 1,058

Miami-Dade Police Department

Classification/Allegation Codes

Code	Type	Description
1	PC	Discourtesy
2	PC	Harassment
3	IA	Harassment/Sexual
4	IA	Harassment/Sex Discrimination
5	PC	Negligence
6	PC	Damage to Property
7	PC	Missing Property
8	PC	Traffic Law Violation
9	IA	False Arrest
10	(Severity)	Departmental Misconduct/Improper Procedure
11	PC	Departmental Misconduct/Improper Investigation
12	(Severity)	Departmental Misconduct/Overreacting
13	PC	Departmental Misconduct/Misinformation
14	PC	Departmental Misconduct/Misrepresentation
15	PC	Departmental Misconduct/Abuse of Authority
16	PC	Departmental Misconduct/Unnecessary Towing
17	(Severity)	Departmental Misconduct/Improper Search
18	IA	Criminal Misconduct/Misdemeanor
19	IA	Criminal Misconduct/Felony
20	IA	Criminal Misconduct/Battery
21	IA	Criminal Misconduct/Theft
22	IA	Criminal Misconduct/Narcotics
23	IA	Criminal Misconduct/Substance Abuse
24	IA	Criminal Misconduct/Bribery
25	(PC)	Minor Force/No Visible Injury (Mere Touching)
26	IA	Minor Force/Injury (During Arrest)
27	IA	Unauthorized Force/No Visible Injury (During Arrest)
28	IA	Unauthorized Force/Injury (During Arrest)
29	IA	Departmental Misconduct/Force Violation
30	(Severity)	Miscellaneous
31	IA	Death in Custody
32	IA	Discrimination
33	IA	Departmental Misconduct/Improper Arrest
34	IA	Departmental Misconduct/Conduct Unbecoming Violation
35	IA	Departmental Misconduct/Property Violation
36	IA	Departmental Misconduct/Substance Violation
37	IA	Departmental Misconduct/Force Violation-Domestic
38	IA	Departmental Misconduct/Battery-Domestic
39	IA	Domestic Related (Used with Other Allegation)
40	SI	Shooting/Contact
41	SI	Shooting/Non-Contact
42	SI	Shooting/Animal
43	SI	Shooting/Accidental
44	(Severity)	Enforcement Profiling

Internal Affairs Matrix—Philadelphia Police Department

Intake

Manner in which complaints can be received:
In person, at district/Unit, mail, letter, Police Advisory Commission, Mayor's Action Center

Anonymous complaints accepted: (yes

Third-party complaints accepted: (Yes)

Penalty of perjury for false statements: (No)

Dispose of complaint prior to classification: (No)

If Y, how?

Complaint forms numbered and tracked: (Yes)

Complaint is forwarded for classification to:

Commanding Officer, Internal Affairs Division (Inspector)

Classification

A complaint can be classified as: Physical abuse, verbal abuse, harassment, lack of service, false arrest, other misconduct, criminal allegation

Once classified, a complaint is assigned to:
IAD investigator or District/Unit Commanding Officer

Investigation

At what command level is each type of complaint investigated: IAD investigator or District Unit Commander

Investigation is supervised/reviewed by: IAD Squad Captain/ Commanding Officer IAD (Inspector)

Recommendation

IA recommends findings (sustained, not sustained, etc.): N/A

If Y, who makes recommendation:

The recommendation is made to:

If Y, who reviews recommendation:

Adjudication

IA makes findings (sustained, not sustained, etc.): (Yes)

Complaints go back through the Chain of Command for adjudication: (Yes)

If Y, who makes final disposition: Police Commissioner

Categories of findings: Sustained, not sustained, unfounded, exonerated, closed without finding due to lack of cooperation, department violations.

Discipline

IA recommends discipline: (No)

If Y, who makes recommendation:

The recommendation is made to:

Discipline is ultimately imposed by:

IA is under what division/office: Internal Affairs report directly to the Police Commissioner

IA is headed by: Deputy Commissioner Richard Ross

Head of IA reports to: Police Commissioner

Rank of IA investigators: Lieutenant and Sergeant

Number of IA investigators: 50 line squad investigators

Total number of sworn employees: 6,679

Internal Affairs Matrix—Phoenix Police Department

Intake

Manner in which complaints can be received: In person, letter, telephone, and e-mail.

Anonymous complaints accepted: (Y)
Third-party complaints accepted: (Y)
Penalty of perjury for false statements: (N)
Dispose of complaint prior to classification: (N)
If Y, how?

Complaint forms numbered and tracked: (Y)
Complaint is forwarded for classification to: Investigator

Classification

A complaint can be classified as: Criminal or Administrative

Once classified, a complaint is assigned to: Investigator

Investigation

At what command level is each type of complaint investigated: For non-supervisory involved, a detective or sergeant/first line supervisor will investigate. If the subject employee is a supervisor, a sergeant or Lieutenant will be primary. If the subject employee is Command or Exec level, the PSB Commander will attend the interview, but the investigation will be completed by a Lieutenant.

Investigation is supervised/reviewed by: Lieutenant, Commander, and Assistant Chief

Recommendation

IA recommends findings (sustained, not sustained, etc.): (Y)
If Y, who makes recommendation: Investigator
The recommendation is made to: Investigations Lieutenant
If Y, who reviews recommendation: PSB Commander

Adjudication

IA makes findings (sustained, not sustained, etc.): (Y)
Complaints go back through the Chain of Command for adjudication: (Y) Employee reviews draft for input before investigation is finalized.
If Y, who makes final disposition: Commander
Categories of findings: Sustained, Unfounded, Exonerated, Unresolved, Policy Failure, Training Issue

Discipline

IA recommends discipline: (Y or N)
If Y, who makes recommendation: N/A
The recommendation is made to: Discipline is based on a discipline matrix solution. For suspensions or greater, a disciplinary review board makes recommendation to Police Chief.

Discipline is ultimately imposed by: Employee's supervisor, Bureau Commander/Administrator, Police Chief

---

IA is under what division/office: Professional Standards Division
IA is headed by: 2 Police Commanders: Cmdr 1- Investigations, Inspections, Mayoral Security: Cmdr 2- Supv Invest., Invest., and Admin.
Head of IA reports to: Assistant Police Chief
Rank of IA investigators: Detective, Sergeant, and Lieutenant
Number of IA investigators: 22
Total number of sworn employees: 3,067

www.ingramcontent.com/pod-product-compliance
Lightning Source LLC
Chambersburg PA
CBHW080522290526

45790CB00006B/2271